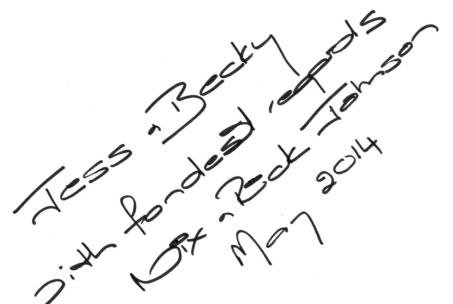

Jess & Becky
with fondest regards
Nix & Rick Johnson
May 2014

A Portrait of
NEW ZEALAND

A Portrait of
NEW ZEALAND

WARREN JACOBS
TEXT BY JILL WORRALL

KOWHAI

CONTENTS

8   **Map of New Zealand**

11   **NORTH ISLAND**

13   **A Volcanic Heritage**

Active volcanoes, boiling mud and steaming geysers. Snow-capped peaks and forest-clad hills surrounding peaceful lakes. Clear trout-laden rivers cascading over waterfalls on their way to the coast.

47   **Nature Tamed**

Rich pastures raising the finest cattle, horses and sheep. Cultivated land producing abundant crops of fruit and vegetables. Vast pine plantations surrounding manmade hydro lakes. Proud cities built around reminders of a pioneer heritage.

73   **The Shape of the Shore**

Sheltered bays dotted with islands – a boat owner's paradise, stormy headlands where oceans meet, beaches with golden or black sands and lined with crimson-bloomed pohutukawa trees.

103   **SOUTH ISLAND**

105   **A Perfection of Grandeur**

Glaciers that approach the sea, mountains eternally snow-clad, alpine glades, tranquil lakes surrounded by bush, waterfalls and crystal-clear rivers gushing seawards.

145   **Order Amidst Natural Beauty**

Plains patterned with shelter belts, high-country farms among the tussock, verdant pastures and plantations, lakes made by human endeavour to harness energy, fine cities and towns lined with European trees and gardens.

169   **Victory of the Sea**

The Moeraki Boulders, Punakaiki's Pancake Rocks, flooded volcanic craters, deep fiords, sandy bays, sheltered harbours and sounds, rocky headlands backed by mountains, river-mouths and tidal estuaries.

SOUTH ISLAND

NEW ZEALAND

Tasman Sea

Pacific Ocean

Cape Farewell

Golden Bay

Marlborough Sounds

TASMAN MOUNTAINS

Tasman Bay

Motueka

Nelson

Picton

RICHMOND RANGE

Blenheim

MARLBOROUGH

Westport

Buller R.

Lake Rotoroa

ST ARNAUD MOUNTAINS

Wairau R.

INLAND KAIKOURA RANGE

Punakaiki

SPENSER MOUNTAINS

SEAWARD KAIKOURA RANGE

Greymouth

Lake Brunner

Kaikoura

Hokitika

Ross

Arthur's Pass

Waikari

Waimakariri R.

WESTLAND

Rakaia R.

Rangitata R.

Lyttelton

CHRISTCHURCH

Banks Peninsula

Fox Glacier
Mt Tasman ▲

Mt ▲ Hooker

▲ Aoraki / Mt Cook

SOUTHERN ALPS

CANTERBURY

Tasman Glacier

Lake Tekapo

Akaroa

Ashburton

Jackson Bay

Haast

BARRIER RANGE

Lake Ohau

Mackenzie Plains

Canterbury Plains

Mt Aspiring ▲

Benmore Dam

Lake Hawea

Timaru

Lake Wanaka

Lindis Pass

Milford Sound

Mitre Peak ▲

Hollyford Valley

Shotover R.

Arrrowtown

Queenstown

OTAGO

Oamaru

Waikouaitia R.

Lake Wakatipu

THE REMARKABLES

Taieri R.

Moeraki Point

FIORDLAND

Lake Te Anau

Otago Peninsula

Lake Manapouri

SOUTHLAND

DUNEDIN

Riverton

Kaitangata

Toko Mouth

Invercargill

Catlins

Bluff

Foveaux Strait

Stewart Island / Rakiura

N

| 0 | | 100 | | 200 km |

| 0 | 50 | | 100 miles |

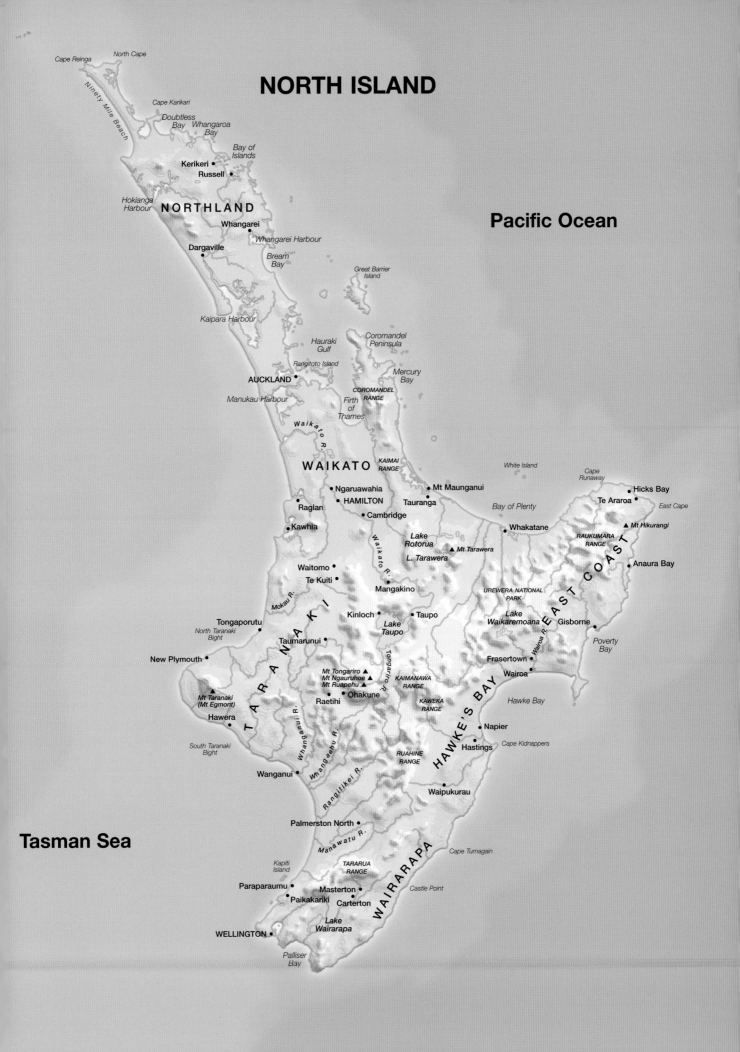

NORTH ISLAND

Pacific Ocean

Tasman Sea

Cape Reinga
North Cape
Ninety Mile Beach
Cape Karikari
Doubtless Bay
Whangaroa Bay
Bay of Islands
Kerikeri
Russell
Hokianga Harbour
NORTHLAND
Whangarei
Whangarei Harbour
Dargaville
Bream Bay
Great Barrier Island
Kaipara Harbour
Hauraki Gulf
Coromandel Peninsula
Rangitoto Island
AUCKLAND
Mercury Bay
Manukau Harbour
COROMANDEL RANGE
Firth of Thames
Waikato R.
WAIKATO
KAIMAI RANGE
White Island
Cape Runaway
Ngaruawahia
Mt Maunganui
Hicks Bay
Te Araroa
East Cape
Raglan
HAMILTON
Tauranga
Bay of Plenty
Cambridge
Whakatane
RAUKUMARA RANGE
Mt Hikurangi
Kawhia
Lake Rotorua
Mt Tarawera
L. Tarawera
Waikato R.
Anaura Bay
Waitomo
Te Kuiti
Mangakino
UREWERA NATIONAL PARK
EAST COAST
Mokau R.
Kinloch
Taupo
Lake Waikaremoana
Gisborne
Tongaporutu
North Taranaki Bight
Lake Taupo
Poverty Bay
New Plymouth
TARANAKI
Taumarunui
Tongariro R.
Frasertown
Wairoa R.
Wairoa
Mt Tongariro
Mt Ngauruhoe
Mt Ruapehu
KAIMANAWA RANGE
Mt Taranaki (Mt Egmont)
Raetihi
Ohakune
KAWEKA RANGE
HAWKE'S BAY
Hawke Bay
Hawera
Whanganui R.
Napier
South Taranaki Bight
Whangaehu R.
RUAHINE RANGE
Hastings
Cape Kidnappers
Wanganui
Rangitikei R.
Waipukurau
Palmerston North
Manawatu R.
Cape Turnagain
WAIRARAPA
Kapiti Island
TARARUA RANGE
Castle Point
Paraparaumu
Masterton
Paikakariki
Carterton
Lake Wairarapa
WELLINGTON
Palliser Bay

NORTH ISLAND

FROM ARCS OF SANDY BEACHES to snow-capped peaks, the North Island presents a complexity of landscapes. From the majesty of the stark volcanic landscape in the centre of the island it's just a few hours' drive to the lively sophistication of Wellington, New Zealand's capital. In the north, stand beneath a stately forest giant, thousands of years old, then take a motorway straight to the multi-cultural heart of the country's largest city, Auckland.

Even in the urban environment, the natural world is never far away. Auckland's harbours and beaches are an integral part of city life; in Rotorua, mud pools bubble just metres from homes; seals loll on Wellington's beaches, sometimes a stone's throw from café patrons.

Climate has played a part in creating the North Island's distinctive character. Subtropical conditions in the north create lushness and a blurring of seasonal variation. Residents talk of the 'winterless' north and the rest of the country listens, often with envy. The eastern seaboard, in the lee of the central ranges, basks in sunshine and grape-growing warmth. In the centre of the island, far from the modifying influence of the sea, the cooler Volcanic Plateau offers ski slopes and stunning alpine scenery.

This is a place of geologically young landscapes; features of a turbulent volcanic past continue in places, while water and wind remorselessly eat away at the landforms. Its human history too is one of flux. The arrival of the Maori saw modifications to the land. Then, when European settlers began stepping ashore in significant numbers in the 19th century, both land and people changed and adapted. Cultures clashed, mixed, redefined. Forests were felled, farms cultivated and towns founded. The North Island, physically and culturally, continues to be a work in progress.

LEFT: Mt Taranaki from North Egmont Chalet.　**ABOVE:** Wellington at dawn.

A Volcanic Heritage

AT FIRST GLANCE at a map, or from the window of an aircraft, the North Island can appear a more tamed landscape than the South Island, an environment where humans have more firmly stamped their mark.

But stand beside a boiling mud pool in Rotorua, watch steam plume from White Island in the Bay of Plenty, or view the volcanic cones in the heart of the North Island, and it will soon be evident that, beneath a sometimes tranquil exterior, awesome natural forces are at work.

New Zealand is a young country in terms of human history and also its geological past, especially in the North Island. The country sits astride two massive tectonic plates, and the constant movement as the Pacific Plate slides under its Australian neighbour has created the North Island's volcanoes, hot springs, geysers and boiling mud pools. Such features are found throughout the Pacific Rim of Fire (as the boundaries of the Pacific Plate are known), but the volcanoes in the Taupo region are some of the most active in the world.

The tallest of these volcanoes, 2797 m Mt Ruapehu, is also the North Island's highest point. It is one of a trio of active volcanoes, along with the classically cone-shaped Ngauruhoe and the multi-cratered Tongariro. Maori mythology provides an equally dramatic explanation of the origins of the volcanoes. Ruaumoko, the god of earthquakes and volcanic fire, was the son of Rangi the sky father and Papa the earth mother. When his parents were forced apart, Ruaumoko sent earthquakes and fire to ward off any human beings who attempted to set foot on her. Another legend describes how one of the North Island's iconic volcanic peaks came to be so far from the centre of the island's volcanic action. Long ago, Mt Taranaki/Egmont lived in the central North Island, but was driven far to the west after an illicit affair with Tongariro's wife, Mt Pihanga. As Tongariro chased him away, Taranaki gouged out the path of the Whanganui River on his flight towards the sea. The mountain now stands

COROMANDEL RANGE, NEAR COROGLEN

Luxuriant native forest studded with tree ferns clothes the deeply incised valleys and sharp ridges that form the Coromandel Range. Reaching 800 m at its highest point, this range once echoed with the sounds of kauri logging and gold mining. Today some kauri remains, including precious young trees, growing alongside rata, rimu and other podocarp trees. The forest is home to many species of unique New Zealand birds, such as tui, native pigeon and grey warbler.

in splendid isolation, an almost perfect cone that has created an alpine retreat set among one of the most intensively farmed regions of New Zealand.

Volcanic eruptions, lava flows, and the deforming movements along the colliding tectonic plates have helped fashion landscapes of exceptionally rugged beauty. The North Island's mountain ranges have been squeezed up by tectonic forces, as have their loftier counterparts, the Southern Alps. These are true wilderness areas, with isolated, unforgiving terrain, often steeped in Maori legend. Sharply incised ridges, narrow ravines and wide snaking rivers present a challenging environment for farming.

Some of the island's most tranquil landscapes, ironically, were born of violent subterranean activity. Lake Taupo, New Zealand's largest lake and an aquatic playground for thousands of visitors each year, covers the scene of one of the most cataclysmic eruptions in the planet's history.

Humans have learned to adapt to life in a land where earthquakes, volcanic rumblings and even the unheralded appearance of a geyser in the back garden are commonplace. For centuries, Maori have used hot pools for cooking and natural therapies. European settlers and Maori united in terror when one of the most fearsome of eruptions in recent history wrought terrible destruction at Mt Tarawera in 1886.

Today, the volcanic and thermal landscapes of the North Island are still treated with respect, but humans have found more ways to harness their energy. Thermal power stations tap into the pent-up heat underground, but most significant of all is the irresistible attraction to visitors.

ABOVE: HUKA FALLS, WAIKATO RIVER

New Zealand's longest river, the Waikato, has a tumultuous passage from Lake Taupo. The river rises on the slopes of Mt Ruapehu, but before it can begin its more sedate journey north into the Tasman Sea it is forced, foaming and surging, through a chasm created by the volcanic forces that are still active today, and then thunders over the 10 m Huka Falls at a rate of 220,000 litres a second. Appropriately, the Maori name for the falls means 'great body of spray'.

ABOVE RIGHT: TONGARIRO RIVER

The Tongariro River is widely regarded as one of the best trout-fishing rivers in the world, and the finest in New Zealand. Famed for its rainbow and brown trout, it attracts an intriguing mix of anglers – locals out with their lines after work can, and do, run into film stars on the river bank. Both groups are in good company – this river has been fished by Zane Grey, the late Queen Mother and former US president Jimmy Carter. The river begins life on the flanks of Mt Ruapehu and flows into Lake Taupo.

BELOW RIGHT: TROUT, RAINBOW SPRINGS, ROTORUA

Rainbow Springs, near Rotorua, with their crystal-clear waters, provide a perfect habitat for wild and captive trout and the water clarity offers ideal viewing conditions for the thousands of visitors who stroll through this nature park every year. The natural pools and the ponds equipped with underwater viewing chambers are fed by water that has filtered through volcanic rock for up to 50 years. Gentle upwellings cause the sands of white pumice and black obsidian to dance in the light.

16

**PREVIOUS PAGE RIGHT:
MANGAWHERO RIVER, NEAR
OHAKUNE**

From the south-western slopes of Mt
Ruapehu, the Mangawhero River sweeps
through a volcanic landscape that still bears
witness to an explosive past. It gathers power
as it sweeps past Raetihi and Ohakune and
finally joins the Whangaehu River, the waters
merging on their way to the Tasman Sea.

**PREVIOUS PAGE ABOVE LEFT:
EVENING LIGHT, MT RUAPEHU**

New Zealand's unique light helps transform
the harsh Volcanic Plateau landscape, with
Mt Ruapehu as its centrepiece, into a rose-
tinted vision. A more fiery palette once
dominated here. Ruapehu, at 2797 m, is one
of a trio of volcanoes that are all still active.
Over the thousands of years of their existence
they have thrown out untold quantities of lava,
ash and gas. These eruptions have created a
ravaged, sterile landscape, the closest New
Zealand comes to a desert environment.

**PREVIOUS PAGE BELOW LEFT:
RAINBOW FALLS, KERIKERI, BAY OF
ISLANDS**

On the lower reaches of the Kerikeri River,
about 5 km upstream from where it flows into
the sea, the tranquil river takes a sudden
dramatic plunge over a 27 m ledge created by
the river eating away at a softer layer of rock
until it reached more formidable strata. Soft
spray often hangs suspended over the falls,
catching the light. This is no new discovery –
Maori named the falls Aniwaniwa, 'the water
of the rainbow'.

ABOVE: HUKA RAPIDS

The awesome power that's on display at the
Huka Falls, on the Waikato River just below
Lake Taupo, is in part generated about 200 m
upstream where the river meets an inclined
shelf of rock and drops sharply before being
confined in a 15 m-wide chasm. The huge
volume of water, now severely restricted, boils
and churns in protest before plunging over the
falls in a maelstrom of foam.

RIGHT: THE WAIROA RIVER

It might be a mere 80 km in length, but the
Wairoa River in Hawke's Bay is part of one of
the most complex river systems in New
Zealand. Draining a catchment area north of
the coastal town of Wairoa, and already
having absorbed several other rivers into its
flow, the river merges again at Frasertown.
Here it joins the Waikaretaheke River that
begins its life in the mysterious, forest-girt
Lake Waikaremoana. Now swelled to a
substantial river, the Wairoa, broad and
smooth-flowing, sweeps across the alluvial
land around Wairoa. In the early decades of
pioneering settlement in the region, before
road and rail linked it with points north and
south, small vessels plied the river and Wairoa
itself served as both a coastal and a river port.

ABOVE LEFT: PANEKIRI BLUFF, LAKE WAIKAREMOANA

The Panekiri Range rises on one side of Lake Waikaremoana, with peaks over 1100 m high, and runs north-eastwards to terminate in this high and dramatic bluff above the lake. This beautiful star-shaped lake lies in the Urewera highlands at an altitude of 614 m, and is surrounded by densely forested mountains. Formed by an ancient rockfall that blocked the path of the Waikaretaheke River, the lake covers about 54 sq km and reaches depths of up to 247 m.

BELOW LEFT: LAKE ROTOKAKAHI, ROTORUA

Lake Rotokakahi (Green Lake) is one of a pair of lakes 11 km south-east of Rotorua on the scenic road that leads to the Buried Village and Lake Tarawera. A narrow neck of tree-covered land separates it from its twin, Tikitapu (Blue Lake). They are aptly named for the distinctive colours of their waters, perhaps less marked now than in the past. Rotokakahi means 'lake of the freshwater mussel'.

ABOVE: MT NGAURUHOE AND WHAKAPAPANUI STREAM

Mt Ngauruhoe is the most symmetrical of the three volcanoes that rise out of the central Volcanic Plateau. At 2291 m, its classic peak is almost always seen with an attendant puff of steam or smoke. Maori legend says that Ngauruhoe was once the slave of a tohunga or priest who arrived to claim the land. As he and his slave were climbing Mt Tongariro, the tohunga did not notice Ngauruhoe succumbing to the cold until he began to suffer. He called upon his sisters in the ancestral homeland of Hawaiki to warm him. They sent fire, which eventually erupted around him, saving his life but too late to revive his slave, who to this day lies frozen in the snow.

23

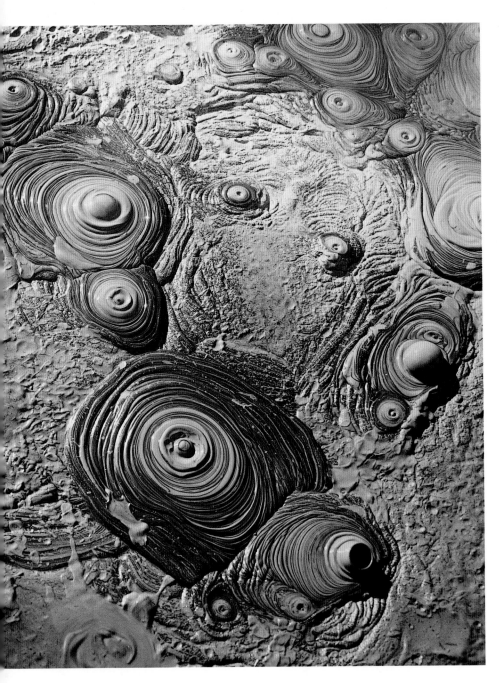

ABOVE: MUD POOLS

Mud pools spit, slurp and gurgle like living beings, fuelled by the thermal activity taking place not far beneath them. The mud is created by acidic gases that break down the rock. Spectators can become mesmerised as the mud forms intriguing shapes, like sloppy clay on a potter's wheel. At Whakarewarewa, one of the best known of the central Volcanic Plateau's thermal areas, Frog Pond is so named because, after rain when the mud is less viscous, it explodes from the multitude of mud bubbles and seems to hop across the surface like tiny silver frogs.

RIGHT: MT NGAURUHOE

Mt Ngauruhoe is thought to have been formed about 2500 years ago and has remained in continuous eruption ever since. Mostly it emits gas in steamy clouds, but on occasions becomes more violent and spews ash. Geological records show that red-hot lava flowed from the summit in 1949 and again in 1954, the flows lasting several months. More recently, in the 1970s the mountain threw out columns of ash-laden gas that climbed as high as 12 km above the mountains. Scientists monitor the mountain constantly and predict that it could become more active at any time.

ABOVE: MT TARAWERA CRATERS

At 12.30 am on 10 June 1886, a series of earthquakes began around Mt Tarawera, south-east of Rotorua. Then at 1.30 am, an explosion occurred on the north-eastern flank of the mountain. Fifteen minutes later a horrendous roar burst from the vicinity of Ruawahia Peak and a vast black column, shot with the glowing red of hot rocks, blasted skywards. Soon, with an even more deafening roar, the south-eastern end of the mountain burst open, throwing up a cloud estimated to have been 10 km high. It was followed by a series of explosions, which could be heard at Coromandel over 160 km away. The eruptions created a long rift of craters and, in the process, killed 155 people and destroyed several settlements.

LEFT: TERRACE FORMATIONS, WHAKAREWAREWA

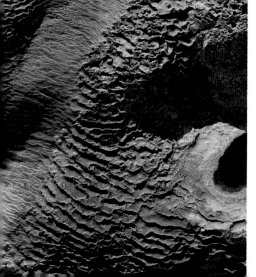

Terraces formed by silvery-white silica, streaked by deposits of a pot-pourri of other minerals, are a feature of the thermal areas. The most famous of them all were the Pink and White Terraces in the Rotomahana Basin, which were destroyed by the Mt Tarawera eruption of 1886.

LEFT: STEAMING CLIFFS, LAKE ROTOMAHANA

In the latter half of the 19th century the Rotomahana Basin, south of Lake Tarawera, with its spectacular Pink and White Terraces, became one of New Zealand's first tourist attractions. Declared one of the natural wonders of the world, it drew visitors from around the globe. But the terraces were blasted into oblivion by the Mt Tarawera eruption that left in its place a lake that still retains evidence of its volcanic beginnings. In places boiling water bubbles up into cold lake water, creating the Steaming Cliffs.

BELOW: MT NGAURUHOE ERUPTING

Always active, Mt Ngauruhoe varies its volcanic displays from delicate plumes of steam to propelling hot debris down its slopes. Here a pall of thick smoke billows away from the vent, set to colour sunsets for days to come and to shower land many kilometres away with a film of fine ash.

ABOVE: CRATERS OF THE MOON, WAIRAKEI

The Wairakei Valley, north of Taupo, is a place of steaming pools and silica terraces that once boasted spectacular geysers. With the tapping of underground steam for the Wairakei Geothermal Power scheme, the geysers no longer erupt. But a new area has opened up, testament to the immensity of the natural forces that are still at work underground. The Craters of the Moon features steaming, bubbling pits and the famed Karapiti Blowhole, an extremely active fumarole.

RIGHT: WAIRAKEI GEOTHERMAL POWER STATION

Steam bores, sunk into the sub-surface cauldron of the Wairakei Valley, tap the vast energy sources of the thermal region, and feed the high-pressure steam to turbines in a power station which produces about 170 MW of power. The generators are housed in a unique building designed to stop the turbine's chamber floors being disturbed significantly during earthquakes.

FAR LEFT: POHUTU GEYSER, WHAKAREWAREWA

Whakarewarewa, one of the most visited of Rotorua's thermal parks, is on the southern edge of the city. Although only 1 km long by 500 m wide, the park contains over 500 hot springs and three geysers. The best known, Pohutu, blasts a column of superheated water at least 30 m into the air. The park has a unique human history too. Local Maori have lived here for more than 100 years, since being displaced by the Tarawera eruption, and still use the hot pools for cooking.

ABOVE LEFT: WHITE ISLAND

New Zealand's most active volcano lies just 50 km from the Bay of Plenty coast. White Island was named by Captain Cook who saw a cloud of white steam as he sailed past in 1769. It is a highly toxic place, with lakes of acid and emissions of poisonous fumes. From 1885 onwards attempts were made to mine the rich deposits of sulphur on the island, but this ended in 1914 after an eruption created a river of boiling mud, or lahar, which consumed about a dozen miners. Today the island is believed to be the only volcanic island in private ownership. Tours visit the island, operators providing their clients with hard hats and gas masks.

BELOW LEFT: CHAMPAGNE POOL, WAIOTAPU

About 30 km south of Rotorua, the Waiotapu Reserve possesses some of the most spectacular thermal activity in the region, including the awesome Lady Knox Geyser, the Frying Pan, Echo Lake, Alum Cliffs and an impressive hot waterfall. The Champagne Pool fills a 3000 sq m explosion crater and is so named because of the colour of the water and the bubbles created by carbon dioxide rising to the surface.

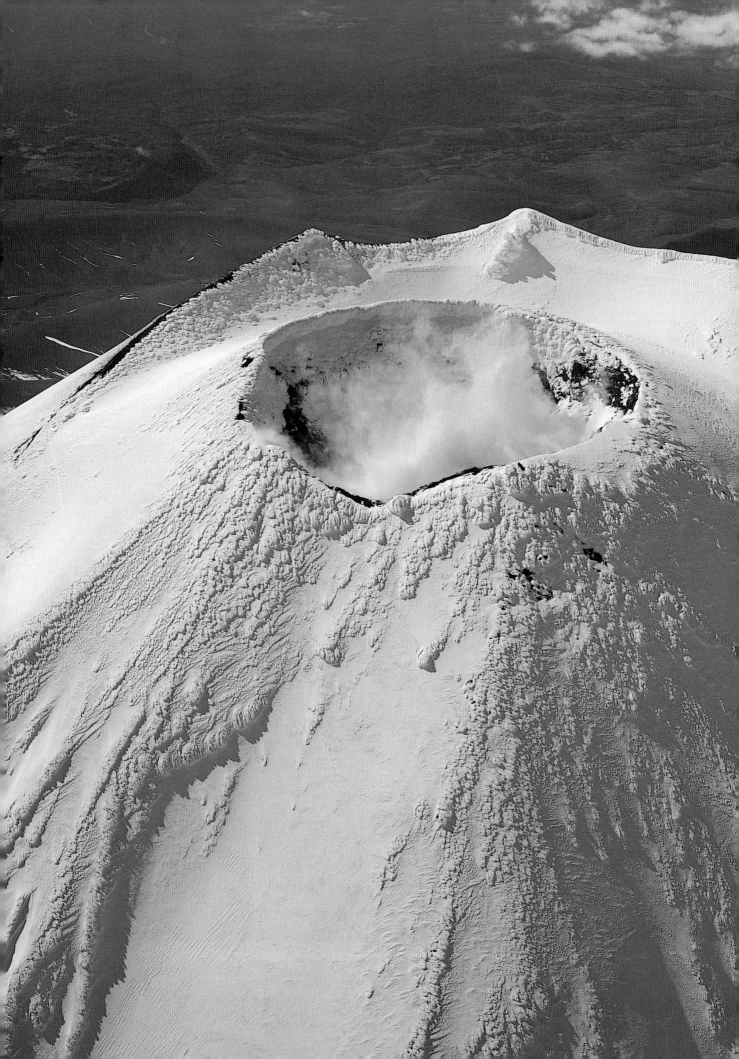

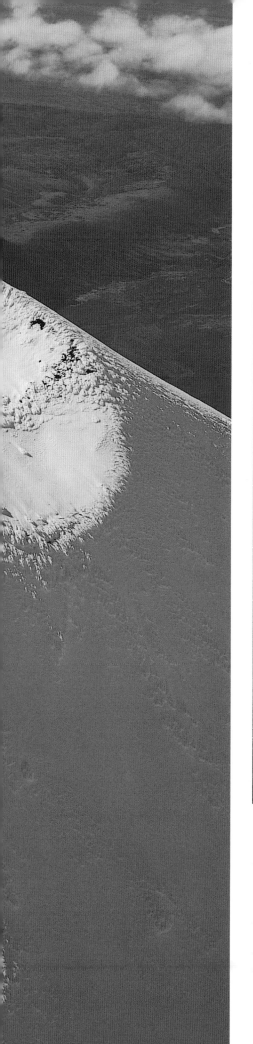

LEFT: THE SUMMIT, MT NGAURUHOE

The beautifully formed cone of Mt Ngauruhoe is a more complex formation than might appear from ground level. Anyone fortunate enough to get close to this active volcano will be able to see that the vent is almost incessantly emitting gas and that ash has formed a crater nestled within a larger snow-filled cavity.

ABOVE: THERMAL ACTIVITY, TIKITERE (HELL'S GATE)

Between Lakes Rotorua and Rotoiti is Tikitere, named Hell's Gate to heighten the already impressive effect of this extremely active volcanic area. The ground at Tikitere shudders and rumbles from the forces that lie pent up beneath ground, and on the surface is more awe-inspiring evidence – sulphurous steam, fumaroles, cauldrons of boiling water and seething mud.

ABOVE RIGHT: MOKAU STREAM AND LAKE WAIKAREMOANA

The Mokau Stream rises on the slopes of the bush-clad mountain Pukepuke, to the north of Lake Waikareiti, and then flows into the Mokau Arm of Lake Waikaremoana. Near where this swiftly flowing stream spills into the lake, it drops over a buttress of rock, creating the Mokau Falls, one of many cascades in the area.

BELOW RIGHT: WAIKARI RIVER, HAWKE'S BAY

Almost halfway between Napier and Wairoa, and about 8 km from the sea in Hawke Bay, is the settlement of Putorino alongside the Waikari River. According to Maori legend the river sprang into being after an explorer in ancient times, Paoa, was passing through the area and his thirsty dog began digging until he found water.

FAR RIGHT: KAURI TREE NEAR RUSSELL, BAY OF ISLANDS

Kauri are the giants of the New Zealand forests, but it was their very size that almost brought about their extinction. The early European arrivals to the bays of Northland, the whalers and traders, quickly realised that the trees, with their massive straight trunks and durable wood, were perfect for masts and spars. The trees were logged relentlessly, with no thought to the fact that the greatest of these trees had taken 1000 years to reach full size. Today the remnant forests of mature kauri have full legal protection.

ABOVE: KOWHAI FLOWERS

Kowhai are often found on forest fringes, river banks and lake shores, and their golden clusters of flowers are irresistible to the New Zealand native bird, the tui. Related to the broom, the kowhai is a legume and is part of the same plant family as the native scarlet kaka beak and the common garden pea.

RIGHT: PAPAKORITO FALLS, WAIKAREMOANA

The Aniwaniwa (rainbow) Stream flows down the Urewera highlands, tumbling over numerous perpendicular outcrops of rock, including the Papakorito Falls. After cascading over the three-tier obstacle, the stream sweeps on until it reaches the beautiful Whanganui-a-parua Arm of Lake Waikaremoana.

ABOVE LEFT: LAKE TARAWERA

Visitors who stand on the shores of the tranquil, bush-fringed Lake Tarawera are hard-pressed to imagine the scene of destruction that would have met them at the same spot if they'd visited in the late 1880s. But, maybe a close look at the strangely truncated mountain at the far end of the lake would provide some clues. Mt Tarawera, made up of 11 domes formed some 700 years ago, erupted on 10 June 1886. Hot ash and pumice rained down for kilometres around, snuffing out human lives and settlements, while the ground shook with terrifying earthquakes. What natural forces destroyed, though, nature is helping to restore as forests regenerate on what was once a blasted, almost lunar landscape.

BELOW LEFT: ACACIA BAY, LAKE TAUPO

New Zealand's largest lake, covering over 600 sq km, is a magnet for boaties and anglers. A moody lake, it was treated with respect by both Maori and early European settlers. Maori believed it was home to a giant taniwha (water monster), a legend that finds a parallel in its geological past. Its waters fill an ancient volcano that, in AD 230, erupted with a force greater than that of Krakatoa. Enough volcanic material was disgorged to cover all of New Zealand and it left much of the North Island a wasteland.

ABOVE: SUNSET OVER LAKE TAUPO AND THE VOLCANOES

Sometimes whipped into rages by winds sweeping across the Volcanic Plateau, Lake Taupo, 369 m above sea level, can be less than hospitable on occasions. But when it shows off its calm side it is easy to see why it has become one of New Zealand's foremost holiday destinations.

ABOVE: MOKAU RIVER, NEAR TE KUITI, KING COUNTRY

It's almost impossible to imagine now that this placid, meandering stream was once one of the busiest waterways in New Zealand. Vessels began sailing the Mokau in the 19th century to ship out coal and timber from the interior and the waterborne trade lasted until the 1930s. The river is regarded as the unofficial border between the King Country and Taranaki.

RIGHT: GLOW-WORM GROTTO, WAITOMO CAVES

Vast limestone reefs slice through the centre of the North Island and stretch for some distance into the South Island. In the Waitomo District of the King Country this limestone country is riddled with underground streams. The best known of these systems is the Waitomo Caves. Living in the darkness of the caves are glow-worms, which are the larval forms of an insect. The glow-worms suspend themselves from the cave roof by a sticky thread that traps insects. Visitors glide through the caves in small boats, and their quiet progress ensures that the view overhead is a mass of tiny blue-white lights.

ABOVE: WHANGANUI RIVER, FROM GENTLE ANNIE HILL

It's not the longest river in New Zealand, and it doesn't carry the largest volume of water, but the Whanganui retains a special place in New Zealand life, past and present. Maori believe the path of the river was gouged out by Mt Taranaki after he was expelled from the volcanic heartland for falling in love with the wife of Mt Tongariro. The river provided a generous source of food for Maori, so was well settled with a series of fortified villages. Later, European arrivals were also attracted to the region. Both regarded the 226 km river as an important waterway linking the centre of the North Island with the Tasman Sea.

ABOVE RIGHT: LAKE WAIKAREMOANA SUNSET

The 'sea of rippling water' is a drowned valley system created by a huge landslide thousands of years ago. But Maori legend offers a much more appropriate explanation for the origins of what is regarded as one of New Zealand's most beautiful lakes. Legend has it that the lake's coves, inlets and islands represent the shape of a murdered girl. She then transformed into a taniwha (spirit or monster) that continues to this day to disturb its waters.

BELOW RIGHT: LAKE TUTIRA, HAWKE'S BAY

Lake Tutira lies in a green basin between Napier and Wairoa. It is a wildlife sanctuary and was once an important food source for Maori. Today it is also popular with anglers as it is well stocked with introduced trout. The lake is separated from its smaller neighbour, Lake Waikapiro, by a small tongue of land, and both drain through a narrow rift into the Waikoau River.

LEFT: CRATER LAKE, MT RUAPEHU

Mt Ruapehu's crater lake is a steaming, sulphurous cauldron, which on occasions disappears completely to be replaced by a vent that belches mud and ash. When it burst through the weakened walls of an ice cave in 1953 it caused one of New Zealand's worst human disasters, when the resulting lahar (volcanic mud flow) wiped out a railway bridge at Tangiwai just before a passenger train was due to cross it – 151 people died.

ABOVE: MT RUAPEHU

Mt Ruapehu's snow-covered slopes offer excellent skiing. With the largest ski areas in the country, the mountain attracts thousands each winter. Few other places in the world offer the chance to ski on an active volcano, seen here erupting in 1995.

Nature Tamed

NEW ZEALAND'S pristine, unique environment was changed irrevocably from the day the first human stepped ashore from a canoe. These first arrivals were Polynesians who brought not only food plants such as kumara, but also dogs and rats. Forests were burned to provide space for villages and crops, the fires often raging out of control. Grasslands replaced trees and some of the country's unique bird species were hunted to extinction. They were easy prey; having evolved in a land free of mammalian predators, many were flightless and had no fear of humans.

These first settlers, the Maori, developed their own unique culture. Villages, built on easily defendable promontories, were fortified with palisades and trenches. The remains of these earthworks can still be seen today. The population was low, however, and resources such as seafood and timber were only harvested to meet immediate needs.

By the time the second wave of migrants arrived, beginning with a trickle of adventurers in the late 18th century and turning into a torrent of settlers in the 19th century, a large Maori population was already living in the North Island. Possession of land became a life and death struggle: to Maori, land has deep spiritual and cultural significance; to the settlers it represented a new life, freedom and the fulfilment of a dream that had been sustained by months aboard sailing ships on perilous seas. In many parts of the North Island bitter land wars dragged on for decades. However, in other regions, Maori and European settlers co-existed more peacefully and newly established towns and villages often relied heavily on Maori farmers for essential food supplies.

Throughout the 19th century, the landscape of the North Island changed dramatically as more immigrants arrived, fuelling the need for land. Forests were cleared, not just to make way for farms and towns but to harvest lucrative timber such as kauri. Settlers were clearing more than half a million hectares of forest a year by the late 1800s. While Maori had a strong emphasis on working with nature to sustain life, the newer

LEFT: PASTORAL SCENE NEAR WAIPUKURAU, HAWKE'S BAY

Gently undulating limestone country has been transformed into lush pastureland in the central Hawke's Bay. This region was once densely forested with native trees, and swamps formerly filled the valley floors, but European settlers carried out extensive logging to create prime grazing, especially for sheep. They also planted exotic trees such as willows and poplars, giving the landscape an almost European feel.

ABOVE: WAIRARAPA PASTORAL SCENE, NEAR MASTERTON

Masterton, at the northern end of the Wairarapa Plain, is the administrative centre of the Wairarapa. The region has a strong agricultural base, a testament to the excellent grazing land on the rolling hills and lush valleys that lie between the Wairarapa Valley and the sea.

RIGHT: FARMLANDS, TARAWERA

The farmlands in the Rotorua region, including around Mt Tarawera, have a more untamed look than many agricultural areas. When European setters first tried to farm this area, they soon lost heart as their animals died of a mysterious complaint, which was labelled 'bush sickness'. The hard-won land reverted to scrub. It was not until the 1930s that scientists discovered the problem was due to a lack of cobalt in the volcanic soils. Since then farming has flourished in the region.

arrivals found the forests threatening and had no qualms about exploiting natural resources for economic gain. Nature was on the back foot.

Cities developed. Auckland began to spread across the narrow isthmus that separated the Waitemata and Manukau harbours, while Wellington was growing around the shores of its own harbour. As roads were few and far between across the wild and often inhospitable interior, settlements sprang up on the coast, sustained by an extensive network of shipping services. Many of the North Island's deep, slow-moving rivers became highways into the interior. Reminders of those early patterns of settlement and transport remain, such as river ports now used only for recreational craft, and lighthouses that once warned sailing ships of perils at sea.

In more recent decades, population drift from the South Island, and even from southern parts of the North Island, has seen the population of the Auckland region boom. The lure of a warmer climate and the emergence of Auckland as the nation's economic powerhouse have fuelled this northward flow. This city is also the largest Polynesian city in the world and is the favoured destination of the thousands of new immigrants who each year choose to make New Zealand their home.

Where populations have expanded dramatically, nature has certainly been tamed, but the kilometres of beaches, sheltered harbours, protected native forests and wilderness areas remain some of the North Island's drawcards for both residents and visitors. Humans have learned to treasure their unique natural environment and step more lightly on the land.

LEFT: AUCKLAND

Auckland is New Zealand's largest and most ethnically diverse centre. About one third of New Zealand's population, some 1.3 million people, lives in the Auckland region, encompassing four cities that merge into one sprawling metropolis. It's not just a cultural melting pot – the area is built around two mountain ranges, three harbours and 48 volcanic cones. And the waters that surround Auckland contain more than 50 islands. The Sky Tower, at 328 m, has become a city icon and is one of the Southern Hemisphere's tallest buildings. For those who find simply admiring the spectacular view from the observation decks too tame, it's possible to bungy jump down the side of the tower, or climb up the tower's mast.

TOP: RANGITOTO AND THE WAITEMATA HARBOUR

Auckland is known as the City of Sails and its residents enjoy the highest ratio of boat ownership in the country. The Waitemata Harbour is one of the favoured places for water-based activities, befitting its Maori name that means 'sparkling waters'. The symmetrical cone of Rangitoto (a 260 m volcano) dominates the harbour views. At just 600 years old, the island is Auckland's youngest volcano, its slopes clothed almost entirely in pohutukawa forest.

ABOVE: AUCKLAND HARBOUR BRIDGE

Built in 1959 and now carrying more than 163,000 vehicles a day, the Auckland Harbour Bridge soars over the Waitemata Harbour that separates downtown Auckland from the North Shore. For a close-up view there are bridge climbs and, for a different perspective of the structure, bungy jumping.

BELOW: DAIRY HERD NEAR CARTERTON, WAIRARAPA

The fertile Wairarapa region offers some prime dairying country, especially in the south, where the land rises to form steep bluffs overlooking Cook Strait. The landscape in this southern district contrasts with the rolling hills to the north. In the west, the terrain is marked by depressions, filled by Lake Wairarapa and Lake Onoke.

RIGHT: LANDSCAPE BETWEEN NEW PLYMOUTH AND MT TARANAKI

The rumpled but fertile and lush farmlands to the north of Taranaki end abruptly at the boundaries of the Egmont National Park. The origin of this distinct line between forest and farm dates back to 1881 when it was decreed that all land within 9.5 km of Mt Taranaki's peak was not to be farmed.

LEFT: THE KAUKATEA VALLEY, NEAR WANGANUI

Although early settlers cleared much of the forest in the Kaukatea Valley and replanted it with imported poplars and conifers, native cabbage trees remain abundant. The cabbage tree is a member of the lily family and probably owes its survival to the fact that its trunk is useless for construction as it consists of tightly packed, coarse fibres. But the plant was nevertheless valuable to earlier visitors. Captain James Cook discovered that the heart of the palm-like foliage could be cooked like cabbage. He produced a variety of sauerkraut with it, one of his many culinary experiments in his efforts to prevent scurvy among his crew.

ABOVE: THE WAIAU VALLEY NEAR WAIROA, HAWKE'S BAY

Shaded by plantings of oak, elm and willow, the lower reaches of the Waiau River contrast sharply with the landforms at its source. Farming and the trappings of civilisation give way to the ranges of the Urewera region, with their dark forests and rugged terrain. Here, the headwaters of the Waiau flow through untamed surroundings.

ABOVE: FARMLAND NEAR LAKE TARAWERA

The Rotorua region supports dairying, sheep and deer farming, along with extensive forestry. Eleven large lakes and several smaller ones provide watery vistas from many farms and forests.

RIGHT: LAKE KARAPIRO, WAIKATO

Formed by a dam on the Waikato River near Cambridge, the long, narrow waterway of Lake Karapiro is set amid lush dairying land. The pride of New Zealand's rowers, the lake is an international-class watersports venue, offering 7.7 sq km of flat water for canoeing, waterskiing and sailing too.

LEFT: WYLIE COTTAGE, GISBORNE

The pioneers in Poverty Bay seldom had time to build large homes. So, although small, some of their cottages are gems of simple but elegant architecture designed to be relatively easy and quick to build. Wylie's Cottage features a shingle roof, a lean-to extension at the rear, and a distinctive style of weatherboarding, where, rather than overlapping, the timber was laid vertically with battens over the joins.

BELOW: THE TREATY HOUSE, WAITANGI, BAY OF ISLANDS

Built in 1883–84, the Residency, as it was originally known, was the home of the first British Resident of New Zealand, Sir James Busby, and his wife Agnes. Its name was changed to the Treaty House by one of its subsequent owners, Lord Bledisloe. The house, designed by the official colonial architect, was largely prefabricated in Australia. On the lawn in front of its elegant French windows, the Treaty of Waitangi was signed in 1840 by representatives of the British Crown and Maori tribes.

FARMLAND NEAR TAUMARUNUI

The King Country is a region of contrasts –
intensively cultivated land and rough hill
country, swathes of native forest, interspersed
with plantings of exotics, and busy service
centres such as the town of Taumarunui.

FAR LEFT: WANGANUI FROM PAPAITI HILL

Wanganui, at the mouth of the Whanganui River, was one of New Zealand's earliest European settlements, and today is renowned for its picturesque parks and private gardens. The city boasts many architectural treasures, including the Durie Hill War Memorial Tower (seen on the skyline at left). What could be a daunting climb to the castellated stone tower is made easy by an earthbound elevator (one of only two in the world) that whisks visitors to the top of the hill.

ABOVE: LANDSCAPE NEAR KINLOCH, TAUPO

Much of the farmland on the pumice soils around the western shores of Lake Taupo has been developed only in recent decades. Several settlements near the lake, such as Kinloch, fill up with holidaymakers in summer, and anglers at other times of the year.

LEFT: PALMERSTON NORTH

Palmerston North spreads across the Rangitikei Plain, some 129 km north of Wellington. It's a crossroads city, at the junction of main routes to and from Taranaki, Hawke's Bay and Auckland. The centre of the city is built around a colourfully planted and manicured square. Once it was not so picturesque, as the railway used to run through this area before it was relocated to the northern outskirts of the city.

LEFT: WELLINGTON CABLE CAR

Since 1902 a cable car has ferried passengers from downtown Wellington to the suburb of Kelburn and the university. The hilltop terminus, with its views over the city, also features a museum devoted to the iconic cable car's history. With suitably flat land in the downtown area scarce, Wellington was quick to adopt the fashion for high-rise buildings, often constructed on sites reclaimed from the harbour. The city centre now leaps upward in towers of steel, glass and concrete.

ABOVE: ORIENTAL BAY, WELLINGTON

Buildings hold tightly to the hillsides above Wellington's harbour. A short stroll from the city centre, Oriental Bay is a picturesque suburb offering cafés, yacht clubs and a boat harbour. City workers frequent its promenade and sandy beach during lunch breaks, and families make it a popular picnic spot at weekends.

ABOVE: Mt Maunganui

Rising beyond a marina, the 223 m extinct volcano of Mauao, situated at the entrance to Tauranga Harbour, is the prominent feature of the resort town of Mt Maunganui. 'The Mount', as it is popularly known, is situated on the narrow neck of a headland that forms the eastern flank of Tauranga Harbour. On the town's seaward side, the wide white-sand beach is one of the country's most popular surfing locations.

RIGHT: Lake Rotoroa, Hamilton

Rotoroa, meaning 'long lake', is a peaceful haven even though it is close to Hamilton's busy downtown centre. Properties with manicured gardens and mature trees line the lakeshore. The lake is home to a population of elegant black swans (the first swans flew to New Zealand from Australia in the 1860s at the same time as they were being introduced for hunting purposes). Native birds are also common in the lake environs.

LEFT: WAIRARAPA LANDSCAPE

When Europeans first arrived in the Wairarapa, the land was clothed in heavy forest – in particular an area known as Seventy Mile Bush. Hardy Scandinavian pioneers who had been allotted land in the district had first to become lumberjacks, felling the forest trees for timber, then building their small communities. As the supplies of timber dwindled, the settlers returned to their original vocation as farmers. Today the land remains some of the most productive in the country.

ABOVE: TRELAWNEY STUD, NEAR CAMBRIDGE

The Waikato's gently rolling hills are ideal for racehorse breeding. The mild climate allows for year-round grazing, which contributes to the horses' remarkable stamina. Many horses that began their lives in this countryside have gone on to become racing legends, both in New Zealand and overseas. But the first association between this country and the horse had little to do with racing. Its first horses were almost certainly troopers' mounts. While the countryside looks peaceful now, it was once a troublesome, restless frontier between the Waikato and the King Country.

OVER PAGE: THE WAIAU VALLEY, NEAR WAIROA, HAWKE'S BAY

A peaceful pastoral landscape unfolds in the valley through which the Waiau River meanders not far from the coast at Wairoa. The river valleys in this East Coast region provide the more accessible farmland in the steeply rising foothills heading inland towards the Urewera ranges.

The Shape of the Shore

THE SEA IS A DOMINANT force in New Zealand, influencing mythology, history, economics, even the physical shape of the land and the psyche of its people. The country has more than 15,000 km of coastline, which in the North Island ranges from sweeping curved bays to heavily indented harbours and inlets, cliffs and vast stretches of sandy beaches.

Mythology and science agree that New Zealand came from the sea. In geological time the land mass has submerged then risen above the waves more than once after it broke away from the ancient continent of Gondwana. According to Maori legend, it was Maui who stood in his canoe (the South Island or Te Waka-a-Maui) and fished up the North Island (Te Ika-a-Maui). Stewart Island was his anchor.

West and east coasts are mostly very different places. The most dramatic evidence of the diverse characteristics of the Pacific Ocean and the Tasman Sea can be found where the two meet, off the northern tip of New Zealand at Cape Reinga. The seas, on their fluid collision course, create a heaving of currents, eddies and white-capped waves.

Typically the Tasman Sea coast is wilder: even on seemingly tranquil days, unceasing long, powerful swells roll in from the west. Kilometres of cliffs and soaring headlands form bastions against the sea, but it continues to gnaw away at the land. Eastern shores are often more sheltered, the Pacific usually calmer. Sandy beaches fill bays, both the vast, like Hawke Bay, and the small, such as those found around the Coromandel Peninsula. The Bay of Islands offers one of the most stunning seascapes in the world.

Even after the long voyage to reach New Zealand, few pioneers turned their backs on the sea. Settlements were mostly established on the coast and

LEFT: PIHA, AUCKLAND

West coast beaches are generally wilder than those on the east coast, and Piha, west of Auckland city, is the quintessential example. Modest baches (holiday cottages) and grand homes alike become insignificant features in this setting of wild grandeur and boisterous surf. Lion Rock, the Piha Stream which flows into the sea by the lion's 'tail', and the bush-clad headland combine to ensure that this landscape continues to be dominated by nature and not by humans, despite its proximity to New Zealand's largest city.

ABOVE: WHANARUA BAY, BAY OF PLENTY

Where the Bay of Plenty coastline heads north-east towards East Cape, it takes a sudden turn due east between Waikawa Point and Otiki Point. Here, the sea's action has created about 12 km of small sheltered northward-facing bays, each fringed with trees on land, and with reefs at sea. One of these is delightful Whanarua Bay, a favourite holiday spot.

RIGHT: KAWAKAWA BAY, EAST CAPE

North of East Cape, and immediately south of Hicks Bay, Kawakawa Bay is typical of the region's coves, with its sandy beach, wave-cut platforms and reefs edged with native bush. In December, pohutukawa blossom blazes scarlet along the coastline. The rocky sea floor here is home to the large packhorse variety of crayfish (rock lobster), a much sought-after delicacy.

often near rivers too. Ports serviced seagoing vessels and river craft. Many Maori pa (fortified villages) were situated near the ocean, as collecting kai moana (seafood) is integral to Maori life. The waters around the North Island remain important fisheries both for local consumption and export.

Improving transport links throughout the North Island saw an expansion of towns inland. But, even today, most of the North Island's major towns and cities sit beside the sea. Workers in Wellington swim and sunbathe at the beach during their lunch break. Aucklanders, who have more than 100 km of coastline within city limits, have the highest ratio of boat ownership in the world. No one in the country lives more than a few hours' drive from the sea, so it is almost inevitable that New Zealanders are renowned for their sporting prowess on the water, whether that be with yachts, kayaks or windsurfers.

Family holidays in a bach (holiday home) at the beach or at a camping ground, shaded by pohutukawa trees fringing the sand, are shared experiences for thousands of New Zealanders. This heritage was almost taken for granted, but today having a home with an ocean view has become more sought after than ever, and is even drawing settlers from far-off shores to find that increasingly expensive 'little place by the sea'.

The sea is more than simply a playground, however, or a source of economic wealth. It is the geographical feature that sets New Zealand apart from the rest of the world, creating the isolation that has helped foster the development of a unique nation.

FAR LEFT: WESTERN COAST OF COROMANDEL PENINSULA FROM KIRITA HILL

Kirita Hill is a 394 m rise overlooking Manaia Harbour and Kirita Bay. It offers a superb view of the Hauraki Gulf, including the offshore islands, Wekarua and Rangipukea. Wekarua means 'nest of the woodhen', which suggests that pre-European Maori had found the islands to be rich in edible bird life.

ABOVE LEFT: MATAURI BAY, NORTHLAND

Sheltered by a lofty headland, Matauri Bay is a glorious 1.5 km stretch of golden sand at the south-eastern end of Whangaroa Harbour on Northland's east coast. The bay is a base for big-game fishing launches as, just 5 km offshore, lie the famed Cavalli Islands, renowned for their stock of game fish.

BELOW LEFT: LONELY COVE, COROMANDEL PENINSULA

Lonely Cove is a short, broad sweep of golden sand backed by tall limestone cliffs and pohutukawa trees. The cove is separated from the grander and more frequented sweep of Cooks Beach by a headland. Its northern end is dominated by a tall bluff on which stands the Captain James Cook Memorial, commemorating the explorer's visit to the area. The monument is inscribed: 'In this bay was anchored 5–15 November, 1769, *HMS Endeavour*, Lieutenant James Cook, Commander. He observed the Transit of Mercury and named this Bay.'

OVER PAGE: MERCURY BAY, COROMANDEL PENINSULA

Mercury Bay is almost triangular, and is lined with lesser bays, inlets and sweeps of sandy beach. Here on 4 November 1769, Cook wrote in his log: 'My reasons for putting in here were the hopes of discovering a good harbour and the desire I had of being in some convenient place to observe the transit of Mercury … If we should be so fortunate as to obtain this Observation the Longitude of this place and Country will thereby be very accurately determined.'

ABOVE: MAITAI BAY, NORTHLAND

The northern end of Doubtless Bay is a
rectangular peninsula, the northern extremity
of which is Cape Karikari. At the base of this
cape, a horseshoe curve of white beach,
backed by rolling countryside, provides an
almost land-locked boat anchorage. Cabbage
trees, tree ferns and nikau palms give the bay
a tropical look.

RIGHT: HOKIANGA HARBOUR

The shallow Hokianga Harbour winds and
twists deep inland, past Opononi and
Omapere, its shores home to small villages
such as Rawene and Kohukohu. Long,
narrow inlets probe between hills dotted with
scrub. This is the scene of some of the
earliest European settlement in New Zealand.
It was here that Baron de Thierry tried to set
up an independent kingdom. On the northern
side the harbour mouth is guarded by
massive, windswept sandhills.

ABOVE: TAEMARO BAY, NORTHLAND

Nestled in a small peninsula east of Doubtless Bay is a pristine bay and beach regarded as one of the most beautiful in the north. Taemaro Bay incorporates an ecological area of regenerating bush and vegetation that has become a significant habitat for kiwi and many other native birds and wildlife.

RIGHT: TONGAPORUTU, TARANAKI

Where the Tongaporutu River flows out into the North Taranaki Bight, some 56 km north of New Plymouth, stand impressive sandstone cliffs, riddled with caverns carved out by the restless Tasman Sea. Just off the southern head, at the river's mouth, is a castle-like rock that was held against attack until 1821 by Ngati Tama warriors. The scenic Tongaporutu River is navigable for about 16 km from its mouth.

ABOVE LEFT: CAPE KIDNAPPERS, HAWKE'S BAY

This sharply incised ridge, which tapers into the sea in a series of rocky outcrops, marks the southern extremity of Hawke Bay. On the crest of the ridge, on two flat platforms devoid of vegetation, are colonies of gannets. The gannet, a relative of the pelican, rarely nests on mainland sites, preferring mostly small steep-sided offshore islands.

LEFT: STATUE OF CAPTAIN COOK, GISBORNE

Captain Cook's visit to Poverty Bay in 1769 was a frustrating one, for he found the Maori there unwilling to trade fresh provisions and reluctant to allow him to replenish supplies of fresh water. This was in complete contrast to the treatment he had received to the north, where the generosity of the inhabitants prompted him to name the region Bay of Plenty. Behind this statue, which stands on Kaiti Hill, is the headland he called Young Nick's Head, after the cabin boy Nicholas Young, the first aboard ship to sight it.

ABOVE: TONGUE POINT, WELLINGTON

Tongue Point, with its narrow shingle beach walled in by steep bluffs and rugged hills, juts into Cook Strait about 6.5 km south-east of Cape Terawhiti and 12 km west of the entrance to Wellington Harbour. It's a place often buffeted by Cook Strait gales. The hills of Marlborough in the South Island can be seen from Tongue Point, slightly hazy with distance, rising up across 40 km of sea.

ABOVE: URQUHARTS BAY, WHANGAREI

Where the Pacific flows into Whangarei Harbour, it swirls around Marsden Point, gouging out a broad curve on the opposite shore, which is called Urquharts Bay. Looking down on the bay is 420 m Manaia Peak, named after a legendary Maori chieftain who sent his principal fighting chief off to battle distant enemies, then stole his wife. The outraged husband returned and attacked Manaia's pa, and chased him, his two children and his faithless wife. Before he could kill them, the gods turned them all into stone, and there they can be seen to this day, pillars of rock on top of the bluff.

RIGHT: ANAURA BAY, EAST COAST

Where forest once stood, now pasture grows, and the whare (Maori dwellings) have been supplanted by a smattering of houses, but Captain Cook would still recognise the cove he visited. He came ashore with a watering party and sat on the hillside above the bay to make a sketch of the sailors filling barrels, and of Pourewa Island, which he called Sporing Island after his assistant naturalist. A small marker now rests on the plateau overlooking the beach, relating how the explorer and his crew gathered supplies and how Joseph Banks and Daniel Solander collected plants that day in October 1769.

ABOVE: KIRITA BAY, COROMANDEL PENINSULA

Kirita Bay looks out across the Firth of Thames towards the ancient volcanic cones that rise up south of Auckland just 26 km away on the other side of the Hauraki Gulf. The whole of the Coromandel's western shore is notched with calm and sheltered bays.

RIGHT: PIERCY ISLAND, BAY OF ISLANDS

The eastern headland of the entrance to the Bay of Islands is a slim finger of land called Cape Brett. Some little distance offshore, looking like a piece of the cape which has been broken off and hurled into the water, stands Piercy Island, better known to thousands of tourists and anglers as The Hole in the Rock. The cavern, which pierces the sharp-topped pinnacle, is lofty enough to allow boats to sail through.

FAR LEFT: TE ARAROA

Spread along the curve of a bay between Hicks Bay and East Cape is the beach and settlement of Te Araroa. This is a favoured holiday spot, with sandy beaches that were once an important coastal highway for Maori. Growing at Te Araroa is a giant pohutukawa tree, thought to be at least 600 years old, that is claimed to be the largest of its species in New Zealand.

ABOVE LEFT: EAST CAPE

On this easternmost finger of land, beyond which there is nothing but a vast expanse of ocean for thousands of kilometres, the hills are eroded and gaunt. Salt-laden sea winds whip along the beaches, bending the gnarled, tough pohutukawa trees and scorching the grass. This is an area with a high Maori population who retain strong links with the land and with their traditions.

BELOW LEFT: POHUTUKAWA FLOWERS

With tenacious roots helping it grip cliffsides, the pohutukawa has found a home along the coast of the upper North Island. The tree is held in great affection by New Zealanders, not least for its blaze of scarlet flowers in early summer, lighting up the coasts before Christmas. There is a legend that when the first Maori arrived in New Zealand, they saw pohutukawa blooming along the shores and promptly threw away the prized but faded red ceremonial feathers they had brought from their tropical homeland. They gathered the flowers as replacements only to find that they faded and fell apart very quickly. Today the trees are the focus of a major conservation programme as they are especially susceptible to the possum, a marsupial introduced from Australia, which has a taste for the leaves and buds.

LEFT: BAY OF ISLANDS, FROM RAWHITI

Rawhiti is an area of scattered farms on the long, tortuous tail of land that terminates at Cape Brett. From the surrounding hilltops there is a panoramic view west and north to the Bay of Islands. Urupukapuka and several smaller islands are dotted through the Albert Channel.

ABOVE: RUSSELL, BAY OF ISLANDS

The now peaceful, historic town of Russell was once known as Kororareka and had a reputation as being 'the hell-hole of the Pacific'. It was a watering hole for whalers, sealers, traders, deserters and runaway convicts and 20 grog shops lined the seafront. It was eventually burnt to the ground in a raid led by two powerful Maori chiefs. Original buildings that survived include the Anglican Christ Church (which is still scarred with bullet holes) and Bishop Pompallier's house, both now fully restored.

LEFT: URUPUKAPUKA ISLAND, BAY OF ISLANDS

In 1770 Captain James Cook gave the Bay of Islands its name, and found it offered 'every kind of refreshments'. Part of the bounty of the bay is the quiet and beauty of numerous bays, beaches and coves. On an inlet on Urupukapuka is the big-game fishing base known as Zane Grey's Camp.

ABOVE: MATAURI BAY HEADLAND, NORTHLAND

This secluded stretch of Northland coast east of Whangaroa is chiefly owned by the local Ngati Kura people. A feature of Matauri Bay is the memorial to the Greenpeace vessel *Rainbow Warrior*, sited on the ridge above the bay, a former Maori pa site. The remains of the boat itself were sunk near the Cavalli Islands offshore from Matauri Bay and have become a popular destination for divers.

ABOVE: GANNET COLONY, CAPE KIDNAPPERS

This colony of Australasian gannets is one of only a few mainland gannet rookeries in the world. The birds, large with yellow heads and black wing-tips, nest from November through December. About 6500 pairs breed here, with numbers increasing considerably since the colony first began to form in the 1870s. At 16 weeks, gannet chicks set off on their maiden flight – an awesome 2800 km odyssey across the Tasman Sea to Australian waters.

ABOVE RIGHT: KARIKARI BAY, NORTHLAND

An ancient volcanic cone dominates the western end of Karikari Bay, dwarfing the surrounding low-lying land with its drifts of sand dunes. Karikari is on the northern side of the peninsula that encloses Doubtless Bay, which was named by Captain Cook.

BELOW RIGHT: CASTLEPOINT LIGHTHOUSE, WAIRARAPA COAST

Reefs, cliffs and a surging sea presented formidable hazards to the vessels that plied this coast during New Zealand's pioneering era. At least 40 ships were wrecked here and 80 lives lost. To improve maritime safety in the area the Castlepoint Lighthouse was built, and still rises like an exclamation mark, perched high on a fossil-rich limestone reef. Captain Cook named the location as the dramatic rock formations reminded him of castle fortifications in England.

PREVIOUS PAGES: MT MAUNGANUI BEACH

Seen from the mountain of Mauao, an ancient Maori fortress, Mt Maunganui's beach curves south-eastwards, fringing the low-lying isthmus that forms one edge of Tauranga's harbour. Once the scene of bloody battles, the well-known Main Beach now hosts thousands of holidaymakers each summer.

LEFT: CAPE REINGA, NORTHLAND

Cape Reinga is one of the northernmost points in New Zealand. It is a place of great significance to Maori, as from here the spirits of the dead are believed to begin their journey to the Polynesian heartland of Hawaiki. It remains tapu (sacred) to this day. The Tasman Sea and Pacific Ocean merge at its tip, sometimes quietly, other times in a tumultuous tangle of waves.

ABOVE: MAKARORI BEACH, EAST CAPE

Makarori Beach is one of several East Cape seaside resorts just north of Gisborne. The warm climate and open sandy beaches, in some places shaded by huge pohutukawa trees, ensure the area is especially busy during summer. Visitors soon discover, though, that if one beach appears too crowded, there are others, such as Wainui, close by.

SOUTH ISLAND

SURF THE PACIFIC at breakfast, soak in a thermal pool in the Southern Alps en route for a glacier walk in the afternoon, and watch the sun plunge into the Tasman Sea at nightfall.

What might sound like a tourism industry fantasy is fact in the South Island. Spectacular things really do come in a small geographical package.

The Southern Alps, including New Zealand's highest peak, Aoraki/Mt Cook, are the island's backbone and the dominant force in the landscape. A once formidable but always spectacular divide between east and west, they dramatically influence the climate.

On the West Coast, rain falls in prodigious quantities, but the east lies in the rain shadow – moss-draped forests give way to tawny grasslands and intricate patterns of cultivation.

The European settlers who came to the South Island discovered a smaller population of Maori than that in the North Island. Although the south was once a Maori stronghold, especially when the huge flightless moa was in ample supply, a high proportion of the indigenous population had moved to the warmer north by the time the next wave of immigrants landed.

The new arrivals came with grand ideas of recreating 'home' in the South Pacific. Christchurch was to be a model English city, and Dunedin a new Edinburgh. These cultural legacies endure, as does the impact of the 19th-century gold rushes that fleetingly saw Otago and Westland become the fledgling nation's economic powerhouses.

A whiff of nostalgia lives on, but so too does a South Island tenacity and vitality, and a passion for a land of stunning contrasts and wild beauty.

LEFT: Evening pastoral scene near Sutton, Otago.   **ABOVE:** Mitre Peak in Milford Sound, Fiordland.

A Perfection of Grandeur

NEW ZEALANDERS HAVE A REPUTATION for sometimes being a little blasé about the awesome landscape that surrounds them. It's hard to deny, when the locals refer to the peaks, glaciers, razor-sharp ridges, alpine meadows and streams simply as 'the high country'.

In the South Island, the high country comprises the Southern Alps, a mountain chain that stretches almost the full length of the 750 km land mass. The highest peak was named Aoraki – the Cloud Piercer – by Maori but is known officially as Aoraki/Mt Cook. Aoraki/Mt Cook is not only a spectacular mountain but also graphically demonstrates the power of the subterranean forces that continue to create the Alps. The mountain was 3764 m high until one December night in 1991 when a landslide swept down the peak, taking with it the top 10 m. Although the event made news around the world, it did not surprise geologists. The Alps are rising up to 10 mm a year, as they sit on the boundaries between two continental plates. These are young and unstable mountains.

There are 27 peaks above 3000 m in the Southern Alps, and the snowfields beneath these feed glaciers that gouge steep-sided valleys. Glaciers once covered much greater expanses of land and, when they retreated, an icy blue chain of alpine lakes was born.

In the south-western extremity of the island, the Alps become a turmoil of sheer rock faces, deep glacier-cut valleys and, where trees can find rootholds, some of the most pristine rainforests in the country. Fiordland was carved out by ice, but its breathtaking beauty today was created when the glaciers retreated and the seas swept in.

The Southern Alps have an immensely significant effect on the climate and thus the cultural and economic landscape. Winds blow warm, moist air across the Tasman Sea, which, when it encounters the Alps, rises and condenses: up to 8 m of rain falls annually in Fiordland. The east of the island lies in the mountains' rain shadow but with more gentle topography and lower rainfall, augmented with irrigation, the land has been more intensely modified by agriculture.

LEFT: SNOWFALL, CRAIGIEBURN RANGE, CANTERBURY

The Craigieburn Range, on the road to Arthur's Pass, is a stark, barren place in summer, but in the winter, when snow covers the bare gravels and scarred rock and dusts the native beech forests like icing sugar, it is transformed into a magical alpine environment.

ABOVE: LAKE TEKAPO, MACKENZIE COUNTRY

A true alpine lake, the waters of Lake Tekapo fill the depression left by an ancient glacier. The lake's unique milky blue colour is caused by the presence of rock flour, which is ground out by the glaciers high in the mountains that encircle its headwaters. Climatic extremes of high summer temperatures and winter snows, combined with low rainfall, make this a tough environment for plants. Tussocks, spiny matagouri and introduced foxgloves eke out a life on the thin soil that overlies the glacial moraine.

RIGHT: GLENDHU BAY, LAKE WANAKA

Autumn is a spectacular season in Central Otago. Deciduous trees, such as these willows that fringe Lake Wanaka, blaze with colour. An alpine region means extremes of temperature, and the chill is a reminder that long ago this area was covered by glacial ice, thousands of metres thick.

While the alpine regions of the South Island exhibit signs of geological youth and raw energy, the landscapes of Central Otago have a time-worn appearance. Metamorphic rock, formed under great heat and pressure, was later subjected to glacial action that has left a rounded topography, punctuated in places by dramatic rocky outcrops. Far from the sea, at least in New Zealand terms, arid Central Otago experiences a more extreme climate, with sun-drenched parched summers followed by freezing winters. Hoar frost can last for days, the eerie whiteness intensified by often cloudless skies.

The South Island's mountainous spine and wildernesses are thinly populated, but, as a consequence of their isolation and magnificence, attract hundreds of thousands of visitors each year. National parks protect a high proportion of these stunning environments but still allow for a vast array of outdoor pursuits.

Opportunities for mountaineering (New Zealand icon Sir Edmund Hillary honed his climbing techniques in the Southern Alps), skiing and tramping abound. Mirroring the natural challenges of the environment, New Zealanders have devised a plethora of extreme outdoor activities to provide a rush of adrenaline for themselves and for visitors. Thrill-seekers are dangled from bungy jumps, hurled over rapids in inflatable rafts and floated off mountain peaks on parachutes and hang-gliders.

No matter how sophisticated the activity or how luxurious the tourist accommodation, the grandeur of the surroundings reigns supreme.

RIGHT: MT TALBOT, FIORDLAND

This high alpine glacial valley was once home to the workers who dug the Homer Tunnel to provide road access to Milford Sound. The tunnelling began in 1935 and the first car drove through in 1945. The workers braved freezing temperatures in their camps, and three men died in avalanches that swept down from the encircling peaks. Rising above the former campsite at Lyttles Flat is 2117 m Mt Talbot, part of the aptly named Barrier Range.

BELOW: AILSA MOUNTAINS, HOLLYFORD VALLEY, FIORDLAND

Just before the Milford Road reaches the Homer Tunnel is a turn-off to the Hollyford Valley. For 17 km a road heads deep into a forested wilderness, one of the most spectacular valleys in the entire vast Fiordland National Park. It's an area favoured by trampers and mountaineers for its remoteness, pristine surroundings and unforgettable scenery.

FAR RIGHT: GLENDHU BAY, LAKE WANAKA

Lake Wanaka has kilometres of indented shoreline, but the spot that has become a special favourite with generations of New Zealand holidaymakers is Glendhu Bay. Just 14 km from the Wanaka township, the bay attracts swimmers, boaties and anglers and sightseers looking for that elusive view of 3027 m Mt Aspiring.

LEFT: BOWEN FALLS, MILFORD SOUND

The Bowen Falls plummet from a hanging glacial valley high above Milford Sound. The two-tier falls plunge eventually into a basin almost perpetually misted with spray. After times of heavy rain (and this is frequent in Fiordland), a walk to the base of the falls leaves visitors saturated but exhilarated by the sheer power of the water.

BELOW: LAKE IANTHE, WESTLAND

Kahikatea and matai forest surround little Lake Ianthe, a gem of a lake 30 km south of Ross. The lake, only 5.6 sq km in area, is fed by forest streams and is estimated to have Westland's largest population of endangered great crested grebe. The lake's romantic name is attributed to a surveyor-explorer who was inspired by Byron's 'Childe Harold's Pilgrimage', a poem dedicated to a child named Ianthe.

FAR LEFT: CLINTON CANYON, MILFORD SOUND

Part of the famous Milford Track winds beside the Clinton River for 23 km. This section is known as the Clinton Canyon, as the mountains rise straight up from the valley floor for about 1200 m, before tapering off more gradually to peaks of more than 1800 m. The canyon climbs up the Mackinnon Pass, through mountain beech, hung with moss, then into alpine meadows where ranunculus and mountain daisy flower in season. This is a favoured home for New Zealand's cheeky and intelligent mountain parrot, the kea.

LEFT: FOX GLACIER

Fed by four small glaciers high in the Southern Alps, the Fox Glacier has a fall of 2600 m on its 13 km journey. In places more than 300 m deep, the glacier is one of the most accessible in the world. The Fox River, which issues from a snow cave at the glacier's terminal face, flows through luxuriant forest before joining the Cook River for a short, tumultuous ride to the Tasman Sea.

ABOVE: THE OKURU RIVER AND SOUTH WESTLAND MOUNTAINS

This range of rugged hills south of Haast is at the southern extremity of the great Southern Alps mountain chain. The snow-fed Okuru River glides through coastal flats, swampy and low-lying, an environment where New Zealand flax and other wetland plants thrive. Where the land is higher, forest, untouched by humans, has taken hold.

113

LEFT: SHOTOVER RIVER AT ARTHUR'S POINT, CENTRAL OTAGO

Drama and contrast characterise the landscapes of Central Otago near Queenstown. In autumn, the colours are especially vivid as poplars and willows burst into fiery golds and oranges, complemented by the emerald greens of patches of irrigated land and the myriad blues from gold-bearing rivers. This is hard land to farm, and introduced species such as broom have spread far and wide, favouring rocky spurs and inaccessible gullies.

ABOVE: HIGH-COUNTRY ROAD NEAR GLENMORE STATION, MACKENZIE COUNTRY

Towards the head of Lake Tekapo, the Godley Peak range rises up from the tawny landscape of tussock and snowgrass. In winter these peaks are covered in snow, but in summer their heavily eroded peaks and flanks are exposed. The shattered gravels eventually reach the valley floors, helping to create the wide, braided Canterbury rivers.

115

ABOVE LEFT: LAKES TEKAPO AND ALEXANDRINA FROM MT JOHN

Two Mackenzie Basin lakes, two different origins. Snow-fed lakes such as Tekapo, filled with glacial flour, are a distinctive blue, but rain-filled lakes such as Lake Alexandrina (to the left) take on green-blue hues. The Mackenzie Basin, named after the Scottish highland shepherd who discovered it (and tried to stock it with stolen sheep), has a high proportion of clear skies and an atmosphere almost free of light pollution. This makes it ideal for astronomical observations, which are carried out at an internationally renowned observatory on Mt John close to Lake Tekapo township.

BELOW LEFT: LAKE TE ANAU

This is the South Island's largest lake. Its western shores are towered over by the densely forested Murchison Mountains, but on the eastern side the landscape is lower, softer and modified by agriculture and the presence of the thriving tourist town of Te Anau. In 1948, two fascinating discoveries were made in the Murchison Mountains. By a small tarn high among the peaks, tracks were detected that led to a bird long thought to be extinct, the takahe. And, near the lakeshore, almost directly beneath the tarn, the legendary but long-hidden Te Ana-Au caves, with their profusion of glow-worms, were uncovered.

ABOVE: LAKE QUILL AND SUTHERLAND FALLS

Cupped in the mountains of the Milford Sound region, Lake Quill pours a steady stream of water to form the Sutherland Falls. These are the highest falls in New Zealand and the third highest in the world. The first leap is 288 m, the second 229 m and the third 103 m. However, when Lake Quill is swollen with floodwaters the falls simply arch out into one spectacular leap of 580 m. The Sutherland Falls are one of the special attractions along the world-famous Milford Track.

LEFT: FOX GLACIER FROM CLEARWATER FLAT

The Clearwater River clatters over stony shallows of a typical Westland river flat. Reflected in its water is a dramatic early evening display of sunlit cloud, which has parted to reveal the icy white of the Fox Glacier.

BELOW: MT TASMAN, FROM FOX, SOUTH WESTLAND

The peaks of the Southern Alps are never more spectacular, or as tantalisingly close, as they are from South Westland. Mt Tasman, 3498 m, New Zealand's second-highest peak, is the source of much of the ice that feeds into the Fox Glacier. Both the Balfour and Albert glaciers begin life in the upper snowfields around Mt Tasman.

LEFT: AORAKI/MT COOK AND SEALY TARN

The Cloud Piercer, Aoraki/Mt Cook is New Zealand's highest mountain. The long ridge of peaks descending to the right forms an impressive wall on one side of the Hooker Glacier. From Sealy Tarn, the glacier appears more like a long river of gravel and boulders, as the visible ice has retreated further up the valley beneath Turner Peak and Proud Pass. These alpine meadows are, in season, studded with the famed Mt Cook lily (above, top) and the mountain daisy (above, lower).

OVER PAGE: LAKE MATHESON, WESTLAND

Lake Matheson, near Fox Glacier in South Westland, is possibly the most photographed lake in New Zealand. There are much larger lakes throughout the country, but it is the mountain reflections that make this body of water special. On a still day the watery images of the Alps, including New Zealand's two highest peaks, Mt Tasman and Aoraki/Mt Cook, are flawless. The lake was once a huge block of ice, marooned as the glacier retreated. The forest that surrounds the lake grows in the low undulating hills of ancient moraine, dropped as the glacier receded into the mountains.

LEFT: WESTLAND BUSH AND STREAM

On the western side of the Southern Alps, where rainfall is frequent and heavy, the bush has an almost tropical luxuriance. Ferns, mosses and lichens cling to the trunks of living trees, creating complex communities of life. When the trees eventually fall, their remains are quickly colonised by even more species, with young trees often germinating from the shelter and nutrients of the rotting wood. It may appear a peaceful scene, but a fight for survival is taking place as the profusion of growth fights for its share of vital sunlight.

BELOW: LAKE BRUNNER FROM LONE TREE LOOKOUT, WESTLAND

The first European to walk the length of the West Coast, in 1842, was explorer Thomas Brunner. This lake was named after him, but the Maori name for Westland's largest lake is more poetic, Moana Kotuku – 'the sea of the white heron'. This rare bird can sometimes still be seen around the lake, which is also rich in trout. Like most other Westland lakes, it too was formed by a retreating glacier.

ABOVE LEFT: SHEEP MUSTERING BENEATH AORAKI/MT COOK, MACKENZIE COUNTRY

In the Canterbury high country, merino sheep graze all summer on the high pastures of the Southern Alps. But as autumn progresses the region's farmers – using horses, sometimes helicopters, but always dogs – head for the hills to bring the sheep down to warmer and less snowy pastures.

BELOW LEFT: SKI PLANE ON TASMAN GLACIER

The Tasman Glacier, sweeping down 29 km from beneath the peak of Mt Elie de Beaumont to the gravelly valley of the Tasman River, was once accessible only to intrepid travellers. But ski planes now offer a breathtaking way for almost everyone to experience the majesty and vastness of a high alpine region by landing on the glacier's névé or snowfield. For the more energetic it's possible to ski down the glacier.

ABOVE: MT ASPIRING, SOUTHERN ALPS

The great spire of Mt Aspiring soars 3027 m high, towering above the surrounding peaks of Stargazer, Mt Joffre, Mt French, Moonraker and Mt Avalanche. A massive national park of 287,205 ha is named after the peak. The Maori name for Aspiring is Tititea – 'the upright glistening one'.

ABOVE: THE LIGHTHOUSE, SKIPPERS ROAD, QUEENSTOWN

The famous – or infamous – road that snakes and climbs precariously through Skippers Canyon leads into a harsh, barren landscape where only a thin layer of soil partially camouflages its hard, rocky skeleton. Some of the rock formations have been given fanciful names, like the Lighthouse, possibly in an attempt to make this inhospitable place feel more familiar, and even a little civilised.

ABOVE RIGHT: REMARKABLES LANDSCAPE, NEAR QUEENSTOWN

Climatic extremes and difficult terrain do not make Central Otago an easy region to farm, but where the landscape relents and produces more expansive, less precipitous slopes, agriculture has taken a hold. With its high sunshine hours and low rainfall, this region now also sports hectares of vineyards, a sight that would have perplexed the early sheep farmers.

BELOW RIGHT: LAKE ALEXANDRINA, MACKENZIE COUNTRY

Lake Alexandrina, close to Lake Tekapo, is a tranquil oasis among the tussock-covered hills. The lake is one of the best fishing spots in the Mackenzie Basin, with rainbow and brown trout in plentiful supply. Small, much-loved baches and boathouses cluster together near the access road, typical of a traditional Kiwi holiday spot.

LEFT: FRANKTON ARM, LAKE WAKATIPU AND THE REMARKABLES

The Frankton Arm of Lake Wakatipu stretches eastwards from the main body of the lake, running beneath the rugged faces of the Remarkables Range and lapping the pine-clad tip of the Kelvin Heights peninsula. The houses in Frankton enjoy proximity to the lake, and are close to the lake outlet, where the Kawarau River begins its spectacular journey through the Kawarau Gorge.

ABOVE: SKIPPERS BRIDGE AND THE UPPER SHOTOVER RIVER

Sparsely populated today, this forbidding mountain country once rang with the sounds of thousands of miners at work. Gold was discovered here in the 1860s and, although some of the workers struck it rich, others lost their lives on the precipitous cliffs, in raging floods and in merciless winter blizzards. Even today, the road to Skippers is regarded as one of New Zealand's most exciting, although some nervous motorists would describe it as completely hair-raising.

131

ABOVE: TASMAN GLACIER SKI-FIELD, SOUTHERN ALPS

Skiing the Tasman Glacier is an 8 km run over a diverse range of terrain. What might appear at first to be a relatively fast downhill run often involves negotiating undulating, challenging terrain that can change from one day to the next. It's not a recommended environment for beginner skiers and an experienced guide accompanies the groups who fly to the head of the ski-field.

RIGHT: HOOKER GLACIER, SOUTHERN ALPS

The Empress, Noeline and Mona glaciers, pushing down from Endeavour Col on the Mt Cook Range, are brought up short by a massive wall of rock, but then join forces, coalescing to become the one great icefall of the Hooker Glacier. This river of ice then makes a comparatively short, steep and spectacular descent towards the valley floor.

ABOVE: TUI TARN, CASS RIVER, MACKENZIE COUNTRY

There are two Cass Rivers in Canterbury, but the best known to trampers is the river that runs down from a high valley between the Liebig and Hall ranges to Lake Tekapo. The still, cold waters of Tui Tarn often reflect the barren, almost subantarctic terrain that characterises these upland alpine spaces.

ABOVE RIGHT: LINDIS PASS HILLS

The Lindis Pass, where a narrow, winding road links the Mackenzie Basin to Central Otago, is a place of extremes. Baking hot and dry in summer, it is often treacherous with ice in winter and sometimes closes completely during heavy snowfalls. No matter what the season, the hills here always appear to have had a covering of rich gold velvet flung over their folds. The pass was known to pre-European Maori, who frequently made use of the 1006 m crossing between the two distinctly different environments.

BELOW RIGHT: LAKE OHAU, MACKENZIE COUNTRY

Like other lakes of glacial origin, Ohau is surrounded by superb mountain scenery. It's the southernmost of the Mackenzie Country lakes and the smallest (60 sq m) but perhaps the most spectacular. High snow-covered ranges rise straight up from the water's edge and, close to a tourist lodge that sits on an expanse of more gentle land, is a ski-field.

PREVIOUS PAGES: PURAKAUNUI FALLS, SOUTH OTAGO

This stunning waterfall is reached by an easy walk from one of the few roads to traverse the Catlins district of South Otago. Although well off most of the major tourist routes in New Zealand, this waterfall is attracting an increasing number of visitors each year and is one of the country's most photographed cascades. The Maori name, which means 'big stack of firewood', is believed to refer to the bodies of Maori warriors, killed in an ancient tribal battle, then stacked ready for cooking and eating.

ABOVE: TREE-FERN FRONDS

In the Westland rainforest, the bulk of the Southern Alps traps easterly flowing clouds causing metres of rain to fall on the narrow strip of land between mountain and sea. In this wet environment tree ferns grow to

prodigious sizes. New Zealand has around 200 species of fern, many of which are found nowhere else in the world. The image of an unfurling fern frond is a common element in Maori art.

RIGHT: LAKE HAWEA, OTAGO

Lake Hawea, lying in the bed of a long-retreated glacier, is about 125 sq km in area and more than 30 km long. Today, the small community at the southern end of the lake is home to a mix of permanent residents and holidaymakers but it was once a Maori settlement. This was wiped out in 1836 by a northern tribal chief and his retinue who had crossed into modern-day Otago from the West Coast, a route now known as the Haast Pass. The highway leading to the pass still follows the western shores of the lake for some distance.

ABOVE LEFT: THE GOWAN RIVER AT LAKE ROTOROA, NELSON LAKES DISTRICT

Tranquil, slow moving – the Gowan River is the picture of a well-behaved river. But after leaving its source at Lake Rotoroa it later joins the Buller River, a waterway that was feared by the European pioneers and is still treated with respect today. The Buller, after rising in the Nelson district, then flows through north Westland, deep and full of dangerous currents and eddies, until it reaches the Tasman Sea at Westport. Lake Rotoroa and nearby Lake Rotoiti are set amid forest-clad mountains and are favourites with anglers, boaties, kayakers and picnickers.

BELOW LEFT: UPPER WAIRAU RIVER, MARLBOROUGH

Marlborough's longest river, the 257 km Wairau begins life as an alpine stream in the Spenser Mountains. This is wilderness area, although kayakers also enjoy the upper reaches. After tracking a south-north path, the Wairau then turns sharply eastwards, following the path of an alpine fault until it reaches the sea in Cook Strait. As its valley widens out, the waters of the Wairau make a vital contribution to the hundreds of hectares of prime vineyard and horticultural land on the Wairau Plains near Blenheim.

ABOVE: UPPER WAIMAKARIRI, CANTERBURY

The upper reaches of the Waimakariri ('cold waters') River are a classic example of a Canterbury braided river system. Rivers, choked with gravels from the fast-eroding Alps, drop their loads as they emerge from the mountains and then have to gouge out constantly shifting channels through the shingle. This river, along with the Rangitata and the Rakaia and smaller waterways, helped build up the Canterbury Plains through this process of transporting and depositing gravel.

141

LEFT: LAKE MARIAN AND MT CROSSCUT

Tucked into the folds of the mountains at the head of the Maria Valley in Fiordland's Hollyford region is Lake Marian. The lake's European name seems hardly to do its awesome setting justice. It was Surveyor General E.H. Wilmot who named the valley and lake after a young cousin. She'd clearly left an impression on Wilmot, who also bestowed variations on her name on two lakes at the head of the nearby Lyttle Falls – Mariana and Marianette.

ABOVE: CRAIGIEBURN VALLEY SKI AREA

In the mountain valleys above the road that leads from Christchurch to Arthur's Pass are several ski-fields, mostly operated by ski clubs. The Craigieburn Valley Ski Area is described as 'steep, deep and cheap', with a series of challenging runs for intermediate and expert skiers, accessed by three rope tows. Keen skiers can stay on the field at homely, rustic ski lodges set in native beech forest. But the fact that the field is only about a 90-minute drive from the city also adds to its attractions for many winter sports enthusiasts.

Order Amidst Natural Beauty

WHEN THE PIONEER SETTLERS stood atop the Bridle Path that linked the port of Lyttelton with the plains of Canterbury, the view must have been daunting. In the distance were mountains far taller than any in England; below were swamps and grasslands bristling with unfamiliar plants and teeming with strange birds. From these unpromising beginnings rose Christchurch, the largest city in the South Island. Founded by the Church of England, the city was planned to be an outpost of Britain in the South Pacific. Sadly, many of the fine stone historic buildings constructed by early settlers using the Gothic style were severely damaged in the terrible earthquakes that struck the Christchurch area in 2010 and 2011, but regeneration plans are in place.

To the south, the Presbyterian Church of Scotland began developing its own city. Dunedin was soon graced by splendid buildings as the city fathers attempted to create a society that would cherish the best of the heritage they had left behind yet which would shed the ills they felt had beset life in Britain.

Faced with an alien environment, it is no wonder that the settlers clung to the familiar and shipped out seeds, plants and animals from the 'old country'. The wealthy, who had acquired vast tracts of land for sheep farms, especially in Canterbury, built themselves mansions, modelled on English country estates. While many of these houses are now of historical importance, many of the live imports caused ecological disasters. In the absence of any natural predators, rabbits reached plague proportions in some parts. The stoats and weasels brought in to control them instead found flightless native birds much easier pickings. The impact of these and other arrivals is still felt today.

LEFT: HIMALAYAN LILY, SOUTH CANTERBURY

The giant Himalayan lilies and rhododendrons, shaded by mature exotic trees, could be a scene straight from an English woodland. But this is Mt Peel station homestead in South Canterbury. Early settlers, confronted with a landscape completely alien to what they'd left behind, often tried to recreate a slice of 'home' with their choice of trees and plants. Many of the original exotic imports had been carefully nursed through long sea journeys from Britain.

145

**ABOVE: DAFFODILS,
CHRISTCHURCH BOTANIC GARDENS**

When the early pioneers first began to lay out
the plan for their new home, they had the
foresight to set aside about 200 ha for a park
and botanical garden. The first tree, an
English oak, was planted in the newly created
garden in 1863. Developed on a site of
wetland and old sand dunes, the gardens are
now regarded as having one of the best
collections of exotic and indigenous plants in
New Zealand. The daffodil woodland was first
established in 1933, and by 1943 more than
500,000 bulbs had been planted, the basis
for the present 2 ha display every spring.

On the West Coast and in Central Otago, gold rushes have marked the
landscape. Shantytowns sprang up rapidly, then disappeared as quickly.
Hokitika's population, once the fifth largest in the country, has halved.

With only about 35 per cent of New Zealanders living in the South
Island (and nearly 40 per cent of those in Christchurch) the most
significant human impact on the South Island landscape is through
agriculture, horticulture and, especially in Marlborough, wine production.

From the air, the Canterbury Plains are a tapestry of crops and pasture
of different hues, and on the West Coast and Southland, verdant pastures
for dairy cows have been created from rainforest and grassland.

The abundant water resources in the South Island mountains have also
been tapped for electricity generation and irrigation. The scale of some of
the hydro-electric schemes was audacious. One of the largest earth dams
in the world was built across the Waitaki River, creating the country's
largest artificial lake, Benmore. Further south in Fiordland, a power plant
was carved into the rock under Lake Manapouri. But, immense though
these projects are, they are dwarfed by the landscapes that surround them.

In Christchurch, roses bloom around sundials inscribed with Latin
motifs but, to the east, the Pacific Ocean rolls unhindered until it breaks
on the coast of South America, and to the west is the snowy bulk of the
Southern Alps. This is not, and never has been, Great Britain revisited.

LEFT: CHALICE SCULPTURE, CATHEDRAL SQUARE, CHRISTCHURCH

A modern chalice sculpture by Neil Dawson befits its site near the Christchurch Cathedral. Christchurch was founded as a Church of England (Anglican) settlement, and the cornerstone of its cathedral was laid in 1864. The project foundered through lack of money and was not completely finished until 1904. It was also decreed that Christchurch should have an English-style public school and a university to provide for the educational as well as spiritual welfare of its residents. The cathedral was largely destroyed by the earthquake of 2011, but there are plans to restore and rebuild it. A temporary transitional 'cardboard' cathedral is under contsruction.

BELOW: CHRISTCHURCH ART GALLERY TE PUNA O WAIWHETU, CHRISTCHURCH

The largest art institution in the South Island, Christchurch Art Gallery Te Puna O Waiwhetu is home to over 6,300 items. With superior engineering, the gallery, which opened in 2003, was designed with safety for its collections in mind. It served its purpose so well that the contemporary structure became the Civil Defence Headquarters during the time of the 2010 and 2011 Christchurch earthquakes; it was one of the few buildings left unscathed in the city's centre.

LEFT: THE CANTERBURY PLAINS

The patchwork of the Canterbury Plains has been created by sheer hard work – intensively cultivated fields, meticulously straight fencelines, often accentuated by dark lines of windbreak trees, and all made possible by the flatness of the terrain. Windbreaks are essential here as the nor-west winds that hurtle down from the mountains are capable of whisking away tonnes of topsoil at a time.

ABOVE: TIMARU'S HARBOUR AND WHARVES

To create a port from a mere indentation in Canterbury's Pacific coast took some prodigious 19th-century engineering. Using horse and dray, pick and shovel, steam winches and primitive explosives, the near-impossible was achieved at Timaru. The task was essential as, although Lyttelton had been the gateway to the fledgling colony, it was a hazardous business transporting goods to the south. The Rakaia and Rangitata rivers were wide and prone to violent floods, and it was some years before they were bridged adequately. Today Timaru port is one of the busiest in the South Island. It handles huge volumes of production from the region's booming dairy industry and is a base for the second-largest fishing fleet in New Zealand.

ABOVE: MARLBOROUGH VINEYARD

Rows of vines march towards the Inland Kaikoura Ranges. Marlborough is one of the sunniest regions in New Zealand, and this, combined with a range of soil types, long autumns and crisp cool winters, has made it one of the world's premier wine-growing regions. Although the industry was established only in the 1970s, the region has fast developed a reputation for the quality of its wines, especially sauvignon blanc. It's now the largest wine-growing area in New Zealand, with more than 3000 ha devoted to grapes.

ABOVE RIGHT: PINE FOREST, WHANGAMOA, NELSON

Vast tracts of pine, planted in regimented rows, clothe the slopes of the rugged hills of the Nelson province. There are more than 100,000 ha of plantations in the region, the majority growing radiata pine. The forestry industry is one of the most important in the region with the wood used both for export and within New Zealand.

BELOW RIGHT: NELSON, FROM QUEBEC ROAD

Nelson nestles into the curve of its bay, sheltered from the south by hills rising steeply behind. It supports a region that contains a lively mix of lifestyles, from horticulturists and viticulturists to aquaculturists and potters. This is one of New Zealand's prime holiday spots as it also boasts some of the highest sunshine hours in the country.

OVER PAGE: OTAGO PENINSULA

There is an echo of old Scotland in the
drystone walls, a blaze of gorse and even the
design of the historic homes on the Otago
Peninsula. On the northern side of the
peninsula is the Otago Harbour, reminiscent of
a Scottish loch with its long, narrow shape. At
the head of the harbour is Dunedin, the city
established by Scots Presbyterians in the
1840s and which still retains its Gaelic links.

PREVIOUS PAGE, LEFT: ALPINE NIGHT, QUEENSTOWN AND LAKE WAKATIPU

The evidence of human settlement around the shores of Lake Wakatipu is particularly dramatic at night. Queenstown is one of New Zealand's premier tourist destinations and, although it is set in a region of high peaks and wilderness, it is renowned for its cosmopolitan lifestyle and sophisticated nightspots, restaurants and hotels. Visitors from all parts of the globe can be found here throughout the year – in winter the attraction is snow sports, with sightseeing and outdoor adventure drawcards throughout the rest of the year.

PREVIOUS PAGE, ABOVE: OLD COACHING INN, SKIPPERS ROAD, QUEENSTOWN

This old inn is a reminder of the early days of European settlement when the journey between Queenstown and Arrowtown was an arduous trip that could take two or three days by coach and horse. Today it's a mere 20-minute drive over a sealed highway.

PREVIOUS PAGE, BELOW: ARROWTOWN

When the leaves start to turn colour in Arrowtown, visitors flock to the tiny historic mining town in increasing numbers. Still lined with many cottages that were home to early miners and the townspeople who serviced the mining communities, the main street has changed little in over 140 years. The first prospectors to arrive here reaped more than 100 kg of gold in just a few weeks.

ABOVE LEFT: QUEENSTOWN, LAKE WAKATIPU AND WALTER PEAK

Although Queenstown is a sophisticated tourist resort, it still holds fast to reminders of its pioneering past. The wharf in the sheltered bay and the historic buildings in the town centre hark back to a time when gold prospectors sailed by the boatload from Kingston on the lake's southern shores to set foot ashore at Queenstown ready to seek their fortunes in the surrounding hills.

ABOVE: ARROW BASIN, NEAR QUEENSTOWN

The miners and their rough and ready shantytowns might be gone and the gold all but worked out, but the farming heritage of the Arrow Basin has stood the test of time. Farmers moved here during the gold rushes, certain in the knowledge that miners needed to eat, no matter what else they did with their hard-won cash. It proved a canny move, as farming has outlived mining by more than a century.

LEFT: OTAGO PENINSULA RURAL SCENE

Those fortunate enough to enter the Otago Harbour by sea are often intrigued to experience a journey from wave-battered cliffs, empty beaches, then scenes of pastoral tranquillity on Otago Peninsula, to the head of the harbour where they find themselves just a short walk from the centre of the South Island's second largest city, Dunedin. The peninsula was once a volcanic island, and the harbour its crater, before a massive eruption blew out one side, allowing seawater to flood in.

BELOW: OTAGO UNIVERSITY, DUNEDIN

Founded in 1869 some 25 years after the beginning of the settlement of Dunedin, the University of Otago is New Zealand's oldest university, its initial roll numbering 81 students. The university has an interesting mix of old and new styles of architecture, and the old administration building is a well-known landmark. Dunedin's university contributes greatly to the city's vitality, its student population driving the thriving local entertainment and arts scene.

ABOVE LEFT: ACHERON ACCOMMODATION HOUSE, MARLBOROUGH

The early settlers found the tussock-covered hills of Marlborough's high country ideal for sheep. With such vast areas to cover, shepherds needed places to stay when they were away from the main station, so accommodation houses, such as this one in Acheron (captured here before it was restored), were built. Few trees grew in this arid, harsh climate, so houses were built of cob – a puddled mixture of clay, chopped tussock and chaff – natural materials that were in good supply.

LOWER LEFT: HEREFORD CATTLE, LAKE HAWEA, OTAGO

Along the western shore of Lake Hawea, terraces of fertile land separate mountain from lakeshore. Although mostly devoted to grazing land now, they were once used for cereal crops. The quality of the grain was such that buyers from all over New Zealand would seek it out.

ABOVE: SHEEP, LAKE JOHNSON, OTAGO

Rolling green downs such as these around the shores of Lake Johnson are not the typical terrain associated with rugged, arid Central Otago. The lake lies in the heart of the Wakatipu region, close to Lake Hayes, and although small in scale it is bigger in reputation as the source of excellent brown and rainbow trout.

161

ABOVE: BENMORE HYDRO DAM AND LAKE

Lake Benmore is New Zealand's largest artificial lake and was created by the damming of the Waitaki River with one of the biggest earth dams in the Southern Hemisphere. This immense project was begun in 1958 and completed in 1965. The lake covers about 75 sq km, making it significantly larger than Wellington harbour. Its 160 km length of indented shorelines provides a highly valued aquatic playground.

RIGHT: EVENING LIGHT, LAKE MAHINERANGI, OTAGO

In the early 20th century, engineers dammed a small stream that wound its way through the Waipori Gorge in the hills west of Dunedin. They created Lake Mahinerangi, which provided water for several power stations. The lake was named after the daughter of a Dunedin mayor.

ABOVE: MOLESWORTH CATTLE DRIVE, MARLBOROUGH

The largest farm in New Zealand, Molesworth Station covers about 180,000 ha and supports the country's largest herd of cattle, 10,000 animals. During the summer muster the cattle are driven along steep ridges, over desolate river flats and down through high passes to the Culverden salesyards to the south. From here the herd is trucked to Christchurch. The land now encompassed by Molesworth was once three vast sheep stations, but the land was overgrazed and then hit by a plague of rabbits. A serious weed invasion completed the ecological disaster. The properties were bought by the government and the land management style changed comprehensively. Sheep were removed and cattle introduced, and as a result the land improved dramatically. Today the station is managed by the Department of Conservation and is open to the public for a limited time each year.

ABOVE RIGHT: SHEEP LEAVING THE YARDS, CANTERBURY

While New Zealand's sheep population has dropped from about 70 million in the 1980s to about 47 million today, this animal still remains of absolute importance to the New Zealand economy. Canterbury, famed for its lamb and wool almost since the first European settlers began farming here, remains a key producer, with about eight million sheep in the region, around 20 per cent of the national total.

LOWER RIGHT: LAKE TEKAPO LANDSCAPE, MACKENZIE COUNTRY

Hay production is vital in the Mackenzie Country, where long, hard winters mean feed for livestock can be in short supply. Plenty of dry, cloudless days during a characteristically hot summer provide local farmers with opportunities to grow much of their own feed, which is then stored in massive round bales.

ABOVE LEFT: KIWIFRUIT ORCHARD, RIWAKA, NELSON

Nelson's high sunshine hours and warm temperatures create perfect conditions for fruit production. Kiwifruit, something of a national icon in New Zealand, grows prolifically here and creates a tapestry of rich greens in the gently rolling hills around Riwaka. Riwaka lies in the north-west of Tasman Bay – beyond here the hills rise steeply, forming the marble mountains that separate this region from remote and beautiful Golden Bay.

BELOW LEFT: SOUTH CANTERBURY RURAL SCENE

Situated at the southern extremity of the vast Canterbury Plains, the terrain in South Canterbury shifts from the expansive flat lands beside the Pacific Ocean into rolling, lusher country inland. This area of gentle limestone country and more craggy rock of volcanic origin rises steadily towards the backbone of the Southern Alps. As the terrain changes, so too do the climate and the land-use, as conditions become more extreme away from the moderating influence of the sea.

ABOVE: PASTORAL SCENE NEAR WAIKARI, NORTH CANTERBURY

Waikari, Hawarden and Culverden are small communities set in rolling upland basins surrounded by high ranges. Threaded by outcrops of limestone, much of this country is fertile and ideal for livestock. But, cut off from the sea by the hills, it is also subject to extremes of temperature – baking hot in summer, and white, frosty and freezing on a winter's morning. Pasture that is verdant in spring can be burnt to a crisp in high summer.

Victory
of the Sea

SOUTH ISLANDERS can start their day paddling in the Pacific Ocean, then drive across one of the three alpine passes that separate east and west coasts, to watch afternoon sunlight gleaming in the Tasman Sea breakers.

The sea, within easy reach of almost the entire population, is an integral part of life, especially in summer. Beach holidays are family traditions, whether basking on the golden sands in Nelson province, or braving the rather more chilly waters that lap the coast of Southland.

Where the sea meets land in Fiordland and Marlborough it has created two of the country's most exceptional landscapes. The deep, peaceful, isolated fiords of Fiordland and the convoluted patterns of peninsulas, headlands and islands of Marlborough Sounds were born of rises in sea levels after the last ice age. In the sounds, the water drowned river valleys; in the remote south-west, it swamped valleys gouged out by glaciers.

The southern ocean also separates New Zealand's third island from what South Islanders parochially call 'The Mainland'. Stewart Island is just a 30-minute flight from Invercargill, New Zealand's most southerly city, or a 60-minute ferry ride from the port of Bluff across Foveaux Strait. But, close though it may be, Stewart Island is a world away in terms of pace of life and its unique environment. Far fewer predators ever reached Stewart Island, so its native bird life is unparalleled and the indigenous forests that clothe most of the island have been subjected to little logging. Kiwi are prolific here, rather than uncommon, and one of the world's rarest parrots, the flightless kakapo, also survives here after being driven to the verge of extinction across the strait. It's possible, by combining a sea cruise (where albatrosses will often follow in the boat's wake) and walks through native forest, to spot over 30 species of bird in one day. Penguins, seals, sea lions and dolphins also inhabit the ocean here.

LEFT: SUNRISE, LYTTELTON HARBOUR

Lyttelton Harbour, once to have been the site of Canterbury's principal city, was named in honour of Lord Lyttelton, the chairman of the Canterbury Association. But the site, on the inner rim of the ancient volcano that created the harbour, was too cramped. Instead Christchurch was built on the other side of the crater's basalt walls. The South Island's principal port, Lyttelton was close to the epicentre of the Christchurch earthquakes of 2010 and 2011 and suffered extensive damage. The smaller settlements around the harbour's edge are holiday retreats and commuter satellites.

ABOVE: THE OTAGO COAST NORTH OF TAIERI MOUTH, OTAGO

Small crescents of beach, rocky reefs and headlands create an ever-changing coastal scene north of Taieri Mouth.

ABOVE RIGHT: ERNEST ISLAND, STEWART ISLAND/RAKIURA

Magnificent Port Pegasus harbour is on the southern side of Stewart Island/Rakiura. Protected from the storms and huge seas of the Southern Ocean by the South Arm, even the waters of this harbour could sometimes prove hazardous, judging by the names bestowed on some of the landmarks, such as Disappointment Cove and Fright Cove. Close to the South Arm lies tiny Ernest Island. Clad in native forest, it is alive with birds and has its own sheltered bay, protected from the worst of the storms that roll in from the south.

BELOW RIGHT: STEWART ISLAND/ RAKIURA, VIEWED FROM COSY NOOK, SOUTHLAND

Cosy Nook is a rare place of well-protected coastline along the often tempestuous and windy Foveaux Strait. The thickly forested ranges of Stewart Island/Rakiura can be seen in the distance on the southern side of the strait.

At the northern extremity of the South Island, forest fringes the coast, as does one of the most popular of New Zealand's many great walking tracks. Although never overcrowded, the Abel Tasman National Park is a magnet for thousands of people each year. Visitors can kayak around a chain of tranquil golden beaches separated by tree-clad headlands, or walk leisurely between bays, cooling off in the crystal-clear water before making the gentle climb over a ridge to another perfect beach.

The South Island's coasts are not always so welcoming of humans at play. Along the West Coast, the Tasman Sea can be ferocious, sending veils of spray over cliffs and stony beaches strewn with bleached white driftwood. Not to be outdone, on the east coast, the Pacific makes landfall at Kaikoura in spectacular style. Rocky coves and islets are favoured haunts of some of the country's largest populations of New Zealand fur seals, once almost hunted to extinction. The continental shelf is narrow here and just off the Kaikoura coast the seafloor plunges to up to 6000 m. Three ocean currents converge and the result is a rich store of food for whales, especially sperm whales. They too were once mercilessly pursued by hunters.

The sight of one of the largest creatures on the planet, its tail flukes silhouetted against the snowy flanks of the steep Kaikoura ranges as it dives, in many ways epitomises the South Island's relationship with the sea. Ocean meeting mountain, wildlife in abundance, and humans rediscovering the art of living in harmony with the natural world.

PREVIOUS PAGES: MITRE PEAK, MILFORD SOUND

The impressive peaks that tower over Milford Sound rise straight out of the deep, cold waters to heights of more than 1500 m. The steepness can make the sound seem narrow, though it is actually up to 5 km wide – more than enough space for ocean-going passenger liners to turn around with ease.

ABOVE: TOKO MOUTH, SOUTH OTAGO

The Toko Stream meanders down to a sandy coast through a reedy wetland to spill into a shallow bay. This has been a traditional summer holiday spot for Otago people for decades – low-key and relaxed, it draws people back year after year with the simple pleasures of swimming, boating and fishing.

RIGHT: COASTAL CLIFFS NEAR KAITANGATA, SOUTH OTAGO

South of Toko Mouth, the sea has eroded the land, leaving steep cliffs and boulder-strewn beaches. There is coal in the hills further inland towards Kaitangata and the sea contains its own bounty. Fish is in good supply, as is a New Zealand delicacy, crayfish (rock lobster), and small-scale fishing operations are based at some river-mouth anchorages and bays.

ABOVE LEFT: OAMARU HARBOUR AND CAPE WANBROW

Now a harbour serving a small fishing fleet and a growing number of recreational vessels, Oamaru was once a busy coastal port. During the 19th century it was vital to the region's economy, shipping out wool and grain from the hinterland. Goods were housed in ornate warehouses near the port and banks, hotels and new industries also gravitated to the area. Many of these buildings, constructed of locally quarried limestone (known as Oamaru stone), have been beautifully restored and incorporated in a historical precinct.

BELOW LEFT: MOERAKI BOULDERS, NORTH OTAGO

Moeraki Beach on North Otago's coast is strewn with distinctive round boulders. The stones are septarian concretions, formed over millions of years in the seabed as crystallisation took place around a central core of a small shell or bone fragment, in a process similar to the creation of a pearl. After the seabed was thrust up, the surrounding soft mudstone was eroded, exposing the boulders. According to Maori legend, the boulders are the gourds thrown ashore from a wrecked ancestral canoe.

ABOVE: KARITANE COAST, OTAGO

Two very different coastal scenes exist on opposite sides of the narrow isthmus linking the Karitane Peninsula with the mainland, near the mouth of the Waikouaiti River. A wide sweep of sandy beach and surf that attracts board riders from throughout Otago faces the Pacific Ocean, and just a short walk away is a sheltered estuary that provides mooring for fishing vessels and yachts. The estuary opens onto the deep curve of Waikouaiti Bay.

PREVIOUS PAGES: SOUTHLAND DAWN, RIVERTON

At the western extremity of the sandy curve of bay between Invercargill's Oreti Beach and the town of Riverton, Howell's Point creates a secure anchorage for a small fishing fleet that operates in the stormy waters of Foveaux Strait. The harbour is a shallow one, created by the estuaries of the Aparima and Pourakino rivers.

ABOVE: PUNAKAIKI SEASCAPE

The Tasman Sea can be wild, lonely and moody where it rolls in to meet the West Coast. South of Punakaiki, ravaged, rocky headlands contrast with beaches strewn with driftwood. On stormy days the breakers pound ashore, leaving a fine spray suspended in the air. On land, the combination of abundant rainfall and warm temperatures has created a subtropical environment where lush vegetation, including exotic-looking nikau palms, thrives.

RIGHT: EARLY MORNING SCENE, EAST COAST OF STEWART ISLAND/RAKIURA

Stewart Island can beguile with its golden sand beaches, crystal-clear waters and luxuriant vegetation. But this is also the most southerly inhabited land in New Zealand. The next significant land mass to the south is the frozen continent of Antarctica, and between the two lie thousands of kilometres of some of the most formidable ocean on the planet.

LEFT: PANCAKE ROCKS, PUNAKAIKI

Wind, rain and sea have combined forces at Punakaiki, near the mouth of the Porari River, to sculpt the remarkable Pancake Rocks. About 30 million years ago, alternating layers of hard and soft limestone were created and later thrust to the surface. The trio of erosional forces then set to work, carving out the remarkable pillars and walls. Wave action has also eaten out massive caverns beneath these rocks, forming heaving, awesome surge pools in which shiny tangles of kelp writhe and wriggle. When sea conditions are just right, air compressed in the caverns by wave action forces tall plumes of seawater high in the air, while the earth rumbles beneath visitors' feet.

ABOVE: JACKSON BAY, SOUTH WESTLAND

Jackson Bay can truly be said to be the end of the road. For motorists driving south down the West Coast it is impossible to drive any further alongside the sea. Beyond the small settlement of Jackson is Fiordland, where mountains rise up straight from the waves. In the 1870s, a mining and fishing town was planned for this spot but the attempt failed. Today, fur seals and penguins outnumber the permanent human population, but it remains a drawcard for visitors in search of isolation and, in season, whitebait.

ABOVE: PORARI RIVER-MOUTH, PUNAKAIKI COAST

The limestone country inland from the Punakaiki coast contains some of the most spectacular walks and kayaking in New Zealand. Towering cliffs, clad in subtropical vegetation, and rivers that flow over sculpted limestone boulders, provide a perfect setting for outdoor activities. The coastline itself is a treasure trove of rock pools, wave-cut platforms and sheltered estuaries.

RIGHT: TAHUNANUI BEACH, NELSON

Throughout Nelson's long, hot summers, Tahunanui Beach on the shores of Tasman Bay is alive with holidaymakers and locals enjoying the wide expanses of sand and some of the safest ocean swimming in the country. But as night falls, it's the coast's feathered residents that are out in force, feeding in the wake of the receding tide.

FAR LEFT: GROVE ARM, QUEEN CHARLOTTE SOUND

Captain Cook named Queen Charlotte Sound during his first visit in January 1770. The beauty of its sheltered waterways and forest-clad hills drew him back on subsequent explorations and he and his ships spent about four months in total anchored here. Today the shores are sought-after locations for holiday homes, but the seafaring tradition lives on – the Marlborough Sounds are some of New Zealanders' favourite boating haunts.

ABOVE: KAIKOURA

Kaikoura, once a thriving whaling town, had by the 1980s settled into life as a small town. In 1989 a whale-watching venture was begun, taking tourists out to sea to marvel at the young male sperm whales frequenting the coast. Kaikoura has boomed yet retained its down-to-earth charm. Whales are not the only gift from the sea for nature lovers – thousands of fur seals live on the rocky coasts, and dolphins are common. A fishing fleet operates from the harbour, with crayfish being a prized harvest. The views are quintessential South Island: mountain, forest, farm and shore.

LEFT: MAORI LEAP CAVES, KAIKOURA

This cave system was discovered in a limestone quarry in 1958. Named after a Maori warrior who leapt from the cliff top to avoid capture (and survived), the cave is hung with stalactites, some stained deep rusty red with iron oxide. There are also stalagmites, cave coral and dark, smoky-coloured chert.

ABOVE: TENNYSON INLET, MARLBOROUGH SOUNDS

Tennyson Inlet, which probes inland from the Tawhitinui Reach, is typical of the Marlborough Sounds – deep, sheltered with sharply incised hillsides, some forested, some clad in grassland, flowing down to small, pristine beaches. Access to many farms and even holiday accommodation is by boat only and, in summer especially, the essential water taxi services are augmented by flotillas of yachts and motorboats, making the most of the sounds' extensive network of waterways.

RIGHT: OKURI BAY AND D'URVILLE ISLAND, MARLBOROUGH SOUNDS

Now separated by the swirling, tumultuous waters of French Pass, the hills of D'Urville Island (rear) and Okuri Bay in the foreground were once part of the same mountain range. But in New Zealand's geological past, these mountain ranges began to sink, allowing the sea to flood in across valley floors, leaving just high ridges and spurs above the water level.

LEFT: MT SHEWELL AND FITZROY BAY, MARLBOROUGH SOUNDS

Fitzroy Bay is a complex harbour with many coves and inlets. The forested triangular peak is Mt Shewell (775 m) and the long spur that slopes into the sea forms the northern shore of the almost land-locked bay. The hillsides are the typical patchwork of vegetation cover in the sounds, exotic and native forest, interspersed with grazing and the occasional clearing for a farm or holiday home.

ABOVE: WHARARIKI BEACH, NEAR CAPE FAREWELL

Whariki Beach can only be reached on foot, but it rewards visitors with some of the most breathtaking coastal scenery in New Zealand. With its rugged offshore islands, caves, and massive wind-sculpted sand dunes it looks spectacular any time of the day, but has a special beauty at sunset. The beach is just to the south of Cape Farewell, which was named by Captain James Cook as he sailed away after his first exploration of New Zealand.

ABOVE: KAIKOURA COAST

The Inland and the Seaward Kaikoura Ranges run parallel courses then drop down abruptly to the sea, south of where the Clarence River pours out from its high valleys. The coast is a rugged rock-bound shore of jagged reefs, swirling kelp and deep little inlets where the crayfish from which it gets its name (Kaikoura means 'feast of crayfish') are still abundant.

FRONT COVER: LAKE HAWEA, OTAGO

This view of the deep blue, crystal clear water of Lake Hawea was taken from the south, near the township. Elevated above the lake in a sunny position, the small town of Hawea is a serene alternative to the bustling tourist spots of Queenstown and Wanaka, although there is an abundance of adventure tourism activities such as skiing and jet boating on the mountains and fast-flowing rivers nearby.

This edition published 2005 by New Holland Publishers (NZ) Ltd
Auckland • Sydney • London • Cape Town

www.newhollandpublishers.co.nz

218 Lake Road, Northcote, Auckland 0627, New Zealand
Unit 1, 66 Gibbes Street, Chatswood, NSW 2067, Australia
86–88 Edgware Road, London, W2 2EA, United Kingdom
Wembley Square, First Floor, Solan Road, Gardens, Cape Town 8001, South Africa

Copyright © 2005 New Holland Publishers (NZ) Ltd

Copyright © in photographs: Warren Jacobs, with the exception of pp 10, 12, 17 (2), 18 (top), 24, 25, 26 (2), 27 (2), 38 (top), 40, 41, 53, 69, 76, 90: Robin Smith and pp 147 (bottom): Andrew Fear
Copyright © in text: Jill Worrall and Errol Brathwaite

ISBN: 978 1 86966 091 8 (hard cover)
ISBN: 978 1 86966 359 9 (soft cover)

First published in 1988 by Kowhai Publishing Ltd and in 1999 by New Holland

Publishing manager: Christine Thomson
Project editor: Dee Murch
Editor: Brian O'Flaherty
Design: Dexter Fry

A catalogue record for this book is available from the National Library of New Zealand

10 9 8

Colour reproduction by SC (Sang Choy) International Pte Ltd, Singapore
Printed in China through Colorcraft Ltd., Hong Kong